Tales from the Caucasus

Captivating Myths and Legends from Circassia, Armenia, and Georgia

© Copyright 2021

This document is geared towards providing exact and reliable information regarding the topic and issue covered. The publication is sold with the idea that the publisher is not required to render accounting, officially permitted, or otherwise, qualified services. If advice is necessary, legal or professional, a practiced individual in the profession should be ordered.

From a Declaration of Principles which was accepted and approved equally by a Committee of the American Bar Association and a Committee of Publishers and Associations.

In no way is it legal to reproduce, duplicate, or transmit any part of this document in either electronic means or in printed format. Recording of this publication is strictly prohibited and any storage of this document is not allowed unless with written permission from the publisher. All rights reserved.

The information provided herein is stated to be truthful and consistent, in that any liability, in terms of inattention or otherwise, by any usage or abuse of any policies, processes, or directions contained within is the solitary and utter responsibility of the recipient reader. Under no circumstances will any legal responsibility or blame be held against the publisher for any reparation, damages, or monetary loss due to the information herein, either directly or indirectly.

Respective authors own all copyrights not held by the publisher.

The information herein is offered for informational purposes solely, and is universal as so. The presentation of the information is without contract or any type of guarantee assurance.

The trademarks that are used are without any consent, and the publication of the trademark is without permission or backing by the trademark owner. All trademarks and brands within this book are for clarifying purposes only and are owned by the owners themselves, not affiliated with this document.

Free Bonus from Captivating History (Available for a Limited time)

Hi History Lovers!

Now you have a chance to join our exclusive history list so you can get your first history ebook for free as well as discounts and a potential to get more history books for free! Simply visit the link below to join.

Captivatinghistory.com/ebook

Also, make sure to follow us on Facebook, Twitter and Youtube by searching for Captivating History.

Contents

INTRODUCTION	1
PART I: MYTHS AND FOLKTALES	5
PART II: NATIONAL EPICS	25
HERE'S ANOTHER BOOK BY MATT CLAYTON THAT YOU MIGHT LIKE	91
FREE BONUS FROM CAPTIVATING HISTORY (AVAILABLE FOR A LIMITED TIME)	92
BIBLIOGRAPHY	93

Introduction

The Caucasus Mountains straddle the isthmus between the Caspian Sea and the Black Sea. The region is at the crossroads of Europe, Central Asia, and the Middle East and is home to multiple cultures with rich histories and rich traditions. These cultures have produced unique myths and legends, which sometimes have taken on board elements from the traditions of the other nations, who, from time to time, have invaded and occupied this geographically strategic region. Although the Caucasus houses many distinct but related cultural groups, today, it is composed of the nations of Georgia, Azerbaijan, and Armenia, and its northernmost portion is part of the Russian Federation. Other Caucasian peoples include the Ossetians, Circassians, Abkhaz, and Chechens.

Various languages are spoken in this region that relate to three different language families. Georgian is a Kartvelian language spoken exclusively in the Caucasus; the Kartvelian languages are unrelated to any other language families. Azeri is a Turkic language spoken in Azerbaijan, while Armenian is an independent branch of the Indo-European language family that includes Slavic, Celtic, Indo-Iranian, and Romance languages.

The Caucasus region's mythology is a combination of native pagan traditions and influences from outside cultures, including ancient Greece and Persia. Christianity's and Islam's arrival also affected storytelling traditions, as did medieval knightly culture and medieval romance. ("Romance" in this sense refers to a lyric epic centered on the deeds of knights and romantic love.) Unfortunately, much Caucasian mythology and literature have been lost because of incursions by outside invaders: Russia engaged in a campaign of genocide in Circassia in the late nineteenth century, and Turkey did the same against the Armenians in the early twentieth. Once the region was absorbed into the Soviet Union, a considerable amount of native culture was purged as part of assimilation.

The oldest layer of myth from the Caucasus is comprised of the Nart sagas. Narts are a race of people around whom these myths are constructed and have many divine and semi-divine attributes. The Nart sagas tell the stories of the ancient Caucasian gods, and although the stories were altered in response to interactions with other cultures, you can still see the original traditions that inspired these myths. Nart sagas come from the northern part of the Caucasus but are not a unified corpus of myths. While the stories share a certain number of heroes, gods, and plots, each culture has its own names for the characters and versions of the tales, some of which are unique to a particular tradition.

The first part of this book contains myths and legends. Two of the stories in this volume are taken from the Circassian Nart corpus: "Sosruko's Sword" and "Tlepsh and Lady Tree." Sosruko is a Caucasian demigod and hero, known as Soslan in some other traditions; here, you have the story of some of Sosruko's childhood deeds. Tlepsh is an ancient Caucasian blacksmith deity associated with metal and metalworking, while Lady Tree would seem to be the embodiment of the world tree that holds all of creation together.

The influence of Persian mythology may be seen in the Armenian tale of Salman and Rostom. The hero Rostom would appear to be a version of the Persian Rostam, though this story is not connected to the Persian *Shahnameh* ("Tales of the Kings") in which the Rostam legends are contained. By contrast, the Armenian Rostom's cousin, Vyjhan, seems to be related to the character of Ohan in "David of Sassoun," the Armenian national epic. Like Ohan, Vyjhan is known for having a preternaturally loud voice.

"The Golden-Headed Fish" is one Armenian tale that has found audiences outside of the Caucasus. In the early twentieth century, folklorist Andrew Lang published a version of this tale in *Olive Fairy Book*.

The second part of this book presents versions of two national epics from the Caucasus. The first of these is a portion of the Armenian epic, "David of Sassoun." As with most hero tales, the protagonist has many superhuman qualities, but David also is very human; he makes mistakes and sometimes doesn't really understand how the world works, but he is committed to protecting the innocent from those who would harm them and is very concerned about establishing fairness, even if his idea of fairness goes against tradition. Full of the usual feats of strength, battles, magical armor, and magical creatures, "David of Sassoun" also revels in humor. We see this especially in David's relationship with his elderly neighbor, who provides him with tongue-lashings and vital information in equal portions, and in David's final battle with the evil Msrah Melik, who keeps asking for do-overs whenever his blows fail to kill David.

To end is an abridged version of the medieval Georgian national epic, "The Knight in the Panther's Skin." Written by poet Shota Rustaveli, "The Knight in the Panther's Skin" originally was a lyric epic in quatrains, participating in the medieval romance tradition. This tale was written after the advent of Christianity and Islam, and so is not part of the native mythological corpus as the tales about Sosruko and Tlepsh. Nevertheless, it is a gripping story, a fairy tale on a grand scale, in which knights go on quests and pine for their lovers when they are parted, and in which a fair damsel is rescued from a tower. You also may see a faint hint of Persian influence in the person of the eponymous knight who, like Rostam, is clad in the skin of a great cat and carries a whip.

Each of these tales has its unique ethos and theme and contains an admixture of native Caucasian myth and connections to outside cultures and religions. They all show a different facet of Caucasian culture and beliefs about heroism, the pursuit of knowledge, loyalty, and love.

Part I: Myths and Folktales

Sosruko's Sword (*Circassia*)

The Nart Sosruko is among the most important heroes in Caucasian myth and legend. Like most heroes, he has an unusual birth. In some versions of the tale, he is born out of a rock (his name literally means "son of a stone") and then taken to the smithy of Tlepsh, the god of blacksmiths, to be finished. Sosruko has superhuman strength and preternatural growth; he is big enough to ride a horse by the time he is one year old.

When Sosruko was still a very young boy, he liked to visit Tlepsh at his forge, and Tlepsh was always happy to see him. One day, Sosruko went to Tlepsh's forge. Tlepsh was hard at work. "Greetings, Sosruko!" Tlepsh said. "My, how you've grown. You'll be almost as big as me soon, and I think you're old enough to help me at my work. Can you pump the bellows for me?"

Sosruko was proud that Tlepsh wanted his help. He went to the bellows and lifted the handle. When he pushed the handle down, the air came out in such a fierce stream that it blew away the fire, tools, and everything else that stood in its path. The only thing that did not move was the anvil because it was buried deep in the ground.

"That's enough of that, my lad. But I want to see how strong you really are. See if you can lift my anvil," Tlepsh said.

Sosruko tried, but he could barely budge the anvil.

"Ah, you still have some growing yet to do, I see. Never fear! You'll be strong enough one day," Tlepsh said.

Every day, Sosruko went to the forge and tried to lift the anvil whenever Tlepsh wasn't looking, and every day he was able to lift it a little bit further out of the ground. Finally, the day came when he was able to lift the anvil all the way up. He decided that he would surprise Tlepsh with this new feat of strength. He went to the forge very early in the morning, picked up the anvil, and put it in front of the forge door.

When Tlepsh arrived later to start his work, he said, "What is this here? Who moved my anvil? Who besides me is strong enough to do that?"

Tlepsh did not receive the answer to his question until the next day, when three young men, all of whom were Narts, came to the forge. One of the young men was carrying a scythe. Sosruko also was at the forge, watching Tlepsh at his work.

"Greetings," Tlepsh said to the visitors. "What brings you to my forge?"

"We want you to help settle an argument," the man carrying the scythe said. "This here is a magic scythe. It does all its work by itself. My brothers each say that the scythe should belong to them, but I say it should be mine. We don't want our quarrel to come to blows, so we hoped you could help us settle it."

"Yes, I will gladly help you. What do you want me to do?"

"Melt down the blade of the scythe and use the metal to turn it into a sword."

"Hm. I could do that, but I don't think your quarrel would end there. You'd just start fighting over the sword instead, and someone will get hurt."

"What other solution is there?" one of the brothers asked.

"How about this: I'll make you each a fine sword, and you give the scythe to me. I'll use the scythe to make a sword for Sosruko here."

"That's not what we want," the man holding the scythe said. "We want you to make a sword for us from this blade."

"I'll do it on one condition."

"Name it," the brothers said.

"I'll make the sword for whoever can lift my anvil and then put it back where it belongs. You can each have three tries."

Now, the young men were quite strong and very proud of it to boot.

Each of them thought, *Surely, I will be the one to lift the anvil and get that sword!*

The first brother laid hold of the anvil and pulled with all his might, but the anvil didn't move. He tried a second time, and a third, with no success.

The second brother took his turn and moved the anvil a little bit, but in his next two tries, he couldn't lift it any higher than the first time.

The third brother went to the anvil and gave a great heave. He was able to lift the anvil almost to his knees, but then he had to drop it. He tried a second and then a third time, but he could not lift the anvil the way Tlepsh told him he should, and now it lay on the floor, where the man had dropped it, out of its place.

"Well, I think that settles it," Tlepsh said. "The scythe is mine, and I'll make fine swords for each of you. Come back in three days. That's when your new swords will be ready."

"Yes, that is fair. We will come back then. Thank you for helping us," the brothers said.

Just then, Sosruko spoke up. "Tlepsh, can I try to lift your anvil?"

The three brothers looked at the young boy and all burst out laughing.

"You must be dreaming," the third brother said. "You're just a small child. How are you going to lift something that even grown men can barely get off the ground?"

"Yes. Why don't you go back home to your mama? Come back when you're a man," the second brother said.

"Don't even try it. You'll surely hurt yourself," the first brother said.

Sosruko listened to the men's laughter and the rude things they said to him. It made him very angry. He stomped over to the anvil and put his arms around it. He picked it up, set it back in the hole where it belonged, and then pushed until the anvil was all the way into the earth and the top of it was level with the forge floor.

Tlepsh, at first, was astonished but then laughed. "Well done, young Sosruko! Now I think I know who moved my anvil yesterday morning!"

The three brothers also wondered at Sosruko's feat. "Well done indeed, little lad! You have well earned a magic sword, and when you grow up, you can be a champion for the Narts!"

Tlepsh and Lady Tree (*Circassia*)

In this story, the smith god Tlepsh goes on a journey, looking for knowledge. He doesn't find what he seeks but learns some other important lessons instead.

In his collection of Nart sagas, translator John Colarosso notes the cosmic import of both Lady Tree and the child she bears to Tlepsh. The child himself is the Milky Way, which is high in the sky only at certain times of the year, while Lady Tree herself is a world tree, a mythical concept shared with cultures such as the ancient Norse and the ancient Maya. Colarosso further observes that the ancient people who made the myth about Tlepsh and Lady Tree might have thought of the Milky Way as a kind of baby sun and that the seven women tasked with looking after Tlepsh's child might represent the Pleiades.

One day, Tlepsh sat moping in his forge. He was trying to think of something new he could make, but he had no ideas.

"I know how to make sickles and scythes, swords and knives, but what else is there? I'm tired of making those things, but I don't know what else there is to make," Tlepsh said.

Just then, Lady Satanaya came walking past the forge.

That's it! I'll ask the Lady. She is very wise. Tlepsh thought.

Tlepsh called out to Lady Satanaya and invited her into the forge. "My Lady, I have a problem, and since you are so very wise, maybe you can help me solve it."

"Maybe," the Lady said, who didn't really want to be there; she was on an errand and in a hurry. "Tell me what you need."

"I want to make something new in my forge, but I have no ideas. Can you think of some things I might make?"

"I'm not sure why you think I can help you. I think you already make plenty of things. Sickles and scythes and swords and knives are very useful, you know."

"Yes, I know that, but I'm bored with making those. What should I do?"

"Well, maybe you should go on a journey. Go to new lands and meet new people. Maybe if you see what they do in other countries, you'll get some ideas."

"Oh, that's a grand plan, thank you! But I've never traveled before. I don't know what I should take with me."

"I don't think you need to worry about food. Everyone knows you and will be glad to share what they have. Wear a good suit of clothes that won't tear or go threadbare easily and a pair of stout shoes. That's really all you need."

"Thank you, my Lady. I'll start right away!"

Tlepsh then made himself a good pair of boots from the finest steel. He slipped them on and started his journey.

Tlepsh was very fast. He could go as far in one day as a normal man could go in a month, and he could go as far in one month as a normal man could go in a year. Tlepsh went on and on, over mountains and across rivers, until he finally came to the sea. He hadn't found what he was looking for yet, so he decided to see whether the people on the other side of the water might help him. He went into the nearby forest and uprooted some trees with his bare hands. He tied them together to make a raft and then pushed the raft into the surf.

After a time, he came to a new land he had never seen before. He beached the raft and went ashore. On the grass just above the beach, a group of beautiful maidens was playing a game. Tlepsh had never seen such beautiful young women. Each of them was perfectly formed, with lovely flowing hair and beautiful voices like musical bells. Tlepsh decided that he must have one of those women for himself, so he ran across the beach and tried to catch one of the girls, but she slipped out of his grasp, laughing. Tlepsh tried to catch one girl after another, but no matter how quickly he moved, they always seemed to be able to get away from him.

Finally, Tlepsh stopped chasing the maidens. "Please, have pity on me and tell me who you are."

"We are the maidens who serve Lady Tree. You have to ask the Lady's permission before you can have one of us. We'll take you to see her now," the girls said.

The maidens led the way, and Tlepsh followed them. Soon they came to a strange being.

"This is Lady Tree. You may speak to her," the maidens said.

Tlepsh looked at Lady Tree. He had never seen anyone like her before. She looked something like a tree and something like a woman, and a very beautiful woman at that. Her roots went deep, deep, deep into the earth, and her hair reached up into the heavens. She had two lovely, maidenly arms and a delightful face.

When Lady Tree beheld Tlepsh, she immediately fell in love with him. She invited him into her house and fed him a good meal. Then, she showed him a place with a soft bed. Tlepsh was very tired from his long journey, so he fell asleep almost at once.

In the small hours of the night, Tlepsh started awake to find Lady Tree standing next to his bed, gazing at him. Tlepsh found her very beautiful, and he desired her. He stood up and tried to put his arms around her, but Lady Tree stepped back.

"Stop! You must not touch me. I am not for a mortal man," Lady Tree said.

"But I am not a mortal man. I am a god."

Then Lady Tree and Tlepsh made love and were very happy.

In the morning, Tlepsh made to leave.

"Don't go! Please stay with me. I love you!" Lady Tree said.

"I must go. I am journeying to find knowledge to bring back to the Narts. I'm going to journey to the end of the earth because that is where the knowledge might be found."

"You don't need to go anywhere to get that knowledge. I have all the knowledge you could ever want right here. My roots go down, down, down to the very center of the earth and always bring secrets back to me. My hair goes up, up, up to the very highest heaven, and I can teach you anything you might want to know about what there is in the skies."

"Maybe, but what I need is the knowledge from the end of the earth."

"This is where you are wrong. The earth has no end. No matter how far you travel, you will never find it. Stay here with me, and gain the knowledge that you seek!"

The Lady pleaded and pleaded with Tlepsh, but he would not listen. He put on his steel shoes and set out on his journey, leaving Lady Tree weeping behind him.

Tlepsh journeyed on and on and on until the soles of his shoes were nearly worn through, but still, he did not come to the end of the earth. He was wearied from his travels and so turned his path back to the home of Lady Tree.

When he arrived, she was there to greet him.

"So, did you find the end of the earth?" the Lady asked.

"No," Tlepsh replied.

"Did you learn anything in your travels?"

"Yes, that the earth has no end."

"Did you learn anything else?"

"Yes, that a man's body can be hard as steel."

"What else did you learn?"

"That the longest, hardest road is the one you have to travel all by yourself."

"Those are good things to have learned, but what of the knowledge you wanted to bring back to the Narts? Did you find that?"

Tlepsh sighed. "No, I didn't find that anywhere. I looked and looked, but it was nowhere to be found."

"That is unfortunate, and it is unfortunate that you did not stay when I asked you to. If you had stayed, I could have taught you everything you wanted to know, everything that you were seeking on your journey. I even could have taught you how to live forever. But now it is too late, and someday you will die. Even so, I have a gift for you." Lady Tree put a tiny infant sun into Tlepsh's arms. "This is the child you gave me before you left. Guard it well and watch it grow. When it is fully grown, it will teach you all the things you want to know."

Tlepsh returned home with his infant son. He showed the child to the Narts.

"Look up into the night sky. Do you see the Milky Way there?" Tlepsh said.

"Yes, we see it," the Narts replied.

"Whenever you go out on a raid, keep it in sight. Then you'll never get lost."

The Narts promised to heed Tlepsh's words. They found seven women to look after the child.

One day, the child went out to play and disappeared. The women noticed he was missing. They searched everywhere but could not find him.

"The child is missing! You must find him!" they told the Narts.

The Narts saddled their horses and went looking for the child, but they had no luck.

"Maybe the child went back to his mother's house. You're the only one who knows the way. Go and look for the child there," they told Tlepsh.

Tlepsh went to the home of Lady Tree, but his child was not there.

"What do we do now?" Tlepsh asked.

"There is nothing you can do. You will just have to wait until he comes back of his own accord. And when he comes back, you will find yourself fortunate. But if he stays away forever, that will be the end of you," Lady Tree replied.

Tlepsh returned home, mourning the loss of his child.

Salman and Rostom *(Armenia)*

This story of a single combat between two fearsome warriors reflects historical ties between Armenia and Persia and functions as a just-so story about the origins of earthquakes and thunder. The hero of this tale, Rostom, clearly is the Persian hero of the same name (Persian Rostam*), and Rostom's father, Chal, clearly is the Persian Zal. The story retold below is unconnected to the Rostam cycle in Ferdowsi's* Shahnameh; *here, Rostom has been co-opted as an Armenian fairytale hero.*

A long time ago, a giant named Salman was the terror of all the lands around. He forced all the people to pay him tribute. If a town or city could not or would not pay the tribute, Salman would go there and kill all the people, destroy their homes and barns, and lay waste their fields.

The only person who dared to refuse to pay Salman was a nobleman named Chal. Chal was very big and strong, but he looked small compared to his son, Rostom. Rostom was a giant of a man and so strong that he could pull whole trees up by their roots. There was only one horse in the whole world who could carry Rostom. This horse was a magical steed who had white hooves.

One day, Chal decided that he would go and see what Salman had been up to. He mounted his horse and set off to look for Salman. Chal journeyed here and there, but he didn't find Salman until, one day, he saw a huge man mounted on a huge horse coming his way up the road. The man had an enormous spear and looked very fierce indeed. Now, Chal had never seen Salman before, so he did not know that this was the person he had been seeking. Nevertheless, Chal was never one to turn down an opportunity to fight, so he set his spear in rest and charged at the huge man. The giant spurred his horse toward Chal, but instead of engaging his spear, he rode right past as though Chal wasn't even there.

Chal was furious. He had never been so insulted. He turned his horse around and threw his spear with all his might at the giant. The spear whizzed past the giant's head, at which the giant turned around, galloped toward Chal, and plucked Chal out of his saddle as though he were a rag doll. Then the giant bound Chal to the belly of his horse and rode for home.

The giant lived in a huge tent that was pitched near a river. He brought Chal inside the tent and nailed his ear to the tent pole. Then Salman went to his bed, laid down, and went to sleep.

Chal was nearly blind with rage.

"He didn't even have the courtesy to tell me who he is," he muttered to himself.

Salman didn't sleep long. When he woke, he said to Chal, "Tell me who you are."

"I am someone from Chal's country," Chal said, thinking it wise not to reveal his true name.

"Oh, that's good." Salman released Chal from the tent pole. "That means you can go to Chal and tell him to send his son Rostom to fight me. I've heard stories about Rostom, and I want to see which of us is stronger. Tell Chal and Rostom that it is Salman who asks this."

Chal went home. He cast himself down in a chair and sighed.

Rostom noticed his father seemed downcast. "What is wrong, father? What happened on your journey?"

"Well, I found Salman all right. The brigand captured me and nailed my ear to the pole of his tent. He told me that he wants to fight you to see who is stronger. He doesn't know I'm your father. I gave him a false name."

"If Salman wants a fight, then he'll have one. He shall pay for the insult he did to you."

Rostom made ready for his journey. He invited his cousin, Vyjhan, to come along. When it was time to leave, Rostom bade farewell to his horse.

Rostom said to Chal, "If I am in any danger, my horse will know and will stamp his hooves. When he does that, tie all my weapons to his saddle and let him come to me."

Rostom and Vyjhan disguised themselves as wandering monks and set off on their journey. Now, just as Rostom was both huge and strong, Vyjhan also was very large, but his strength was in his voice, not his arms. If Vyjhan cried out, people could hear him on the other side of the country, even if mountains stood in the way.

Vyjhan and Rostom traveled all through that day, and when the sun began to set, they made camp near a small town. In the middle of the night, Vyjhan was awakened by the noise of people lamenting. He went into the village and there saw all the people crying and tearing their clothes.

Vyjhan went up to one of the villagers and asked, "What has happened? Has someone died? Has some disaster overtaken you?"

"The disaster hasn't happened yet, but it will soon. We owe tribute to the giant Salman. We haven't paid it for seven years, but just now he told us we have to have the whole amount ready by morning or he'll kill us all and destroy our village!" the villager replied.

The people worked very hard, and by daybreak, the tribute was ready. Vyjhan saw them arguing over who should be the one to give Salman the tribute. No one wanted to do it because Salman took both the tribute and the person giving it, and the person was never seen again.

"Why don't you let me give the tribute? I'm not afraid," Vyjhan said.

Soon enough, Salman came to the village. He collected all the tribute and scooped up Vyjhan along with it. He took Vyjhan to his tent and nailed his ear to the tent pole.

Vyjhan called out, "Rostom! Help! Salman has captured me!"

Vyjhan's loud cry woke Rostom from sleep. Rostom ran to the village and asked what happened.

"Salman took your friend to his tent by the river. Don't bother to go after him. There's no way Salman can be defeated. Mourn your friend and go home," the villagers said.

No sooner had the villagers told Rostom their tale than Rostom's faithful horse galloped to his side. The horse was saddled, and all of Rostom's weapons and armor were there. Rostom put on his armor, mounted his horse, and galloped to the river.

When he arrived at Salman's tent, he shouted, "Salman! Come out and face me! It is I, Rostom. Let us see who is stronger!"

Salman came out of the tent armed and ready for battle. The two giants fought with spears until nothing was left of the shafts but splinters. Then they drew their swords and fought until their shields were cut to ribbons and their swords were shattered. When all their weapons were broken, they grappled and wrestled this way and that, but neither one could get the upper hand.

Salman and Rostom are still wrestling today. When one of them throws the other, it makes the ground shake, and Vyjhan's booming call can still be heard from time to time throughout the world.

The Golden-Headed Fish (*Armenia*)

This Armenian folktale does not deal with ancient gods or heroes but is closer to a fairy tale, following the adventures of a disgraced prince accompanied by a magical being. This story's function is entertainment, but it also has a strong moral core on the virtues of mercy, loyalty, and repayment of debt.

There once was a king who found his eyesight failing. All of the most learned doctors from all corners of the kingdom were summoned to treat the king, but none could find a cure. Word came to the king that one doctor in a far country was even more learned than all of those in the whole kingdom put together.

"Go and fetch this doctor. Bring him here straight away. He is my last hope," the king said.

The messengers found the doctor and brought him back to the king's court.

The doctor examined the king and said, "There is a cure for your malady. It requires the blood of the golden-headed fish. If I smear some of that on your eyes, you will see again. I will stay here for one hundred days. If by the end of that time you have not found the fish, I must go back to my home."

Now, the king only had one child, a son, who loved his father dearly. The prince had been at his father's bedside when the doctor told the king what the cure could be. The prince begged for the opportunity to go fishing, for he wanted to be the one to restore his father's sight if he could. The king gave permission, and soon the prince and his companions had put to sea.

Day after day, they cast their nets, and day after day, they failed to catch the fish. Ninety days came and went, and then ninety-eight, and on the ninety-ninth day, they fished and fished until the sun was nearly setting, and still no golden-headed fish. The prince and his companions were downcast.

One of the companions said, "I think this task is impossible. Maybe that doctor was telling a story to make fools of us and his majesty the king. We should go home before it gets dark."

"Maybe you're right, but I'll not turn for home until we've cast our nets one last time. Maybe we'll be lucky," the prince said.

And so, the prince and his companions cast their nets and hauled them back in again, and what should they find among the catch but a golden-headed fish! The men placed the fish inside a barrel full of water and put the barrel in the prince's cabin. Then they sailed for home, singing all the way.

While they were sailing home, the prince went to look at the marvelous fish. He gasped with astonishment when the fish put its head above the water and began to speak.

"I know you are a prince. I am a prince too. Please throw me back into the sea. You will have a great reward if you save my life," the fish said.

The prince wavered, but the fish pleaded in such piteous tones and gazed at him with such piteous eyes that the prince took the fish out of the barrel and tossed it back into the sea.

The prince's friends saw what he had done and cried out, "What are you doing? We fished for ninety-nine days to catch that fish! What is your royal father going to say?"

But the prince would only answer, "I have my reasons," and said no more.

When the prince and his companions arrived back at the palace, the companions told the king what the prince had done.

"How dare you! How dare you take from me the one chance I had for a cure. Tomorrow I will hang you as a criminal! You are no son of mine!" the king shouted.

The queen heard what the king said, so she quickly spirited the prince away and put clothes on him that made him look like a commoner. She gave him a purse full of gold and jewels and sent him to the harbor to find passage on whichever ship was sailing farthest away. With many tears, mother and son bid farewell to one another, and soon the prince was at sea again, thinking that, this time, he would never return.

The prince disembarked on the distant island the ship brought him to. He found a pleasant cottage to live in and soon desired a servant to wait upon him. He sent out word that he was looking for such a servant, and the next day, there was a line of men outside his door hoping to get the position. The prince interviewed one after the other, and at the end of the interview, he asked them what wages they desired. Everyone answered with a sum of money that they said must be paid at the end of every month. Although the prince thought that any one of the men would do as a servant, he also had the nagging feeling that he hadn't found the right man yet, so he continued interviewing one man after another.

At the end of a very long day, there was finally only one candidate left.

The prince spoke with him about his qualifications, and as he had done so many times before, he said, "What do you expect for wages?"

"I don't need to be paid, sir, at least not yet. Let me serve you for a time, and if you think me worth paying, you can reward me then," the man replied.

The prince was intrigued by this and told the man that he was hired.

The two lived together peaceably for a time, but then one day, terror came to their little island. A dragon took up residence not far away, and it had begun raiding cattle pens and sheepfolds.

"What shall we do? Once the dragon eats all our sheep and cattle, it will eat our children, and then it will surely eat us!" the people lamented.

The king of the island sent some soldiers on an expedition to kill the dragon. When none of them came back, he sent another group of soldiers, and then another, and then another, but none of them came back alive. In despair, the king proclaimed that anyone who killed the dragon would get half his kingdom and the hand of his daughter in marriage.

The servant heard the proclamation. Without saying anything to the prince, he went to the palace and asked for an audience with the king.

"My master can kill that dragon. Will you keep your word and reward him as you said?" the servant said.

"I most certainly will. That dragon has already eaten half my army. Anyone who can kill that beast deserves that kind of reward," the king replied.

That night, the servant slipped quietly out of the house and went to the place where the dragon lived. When it came slithering out of its den, the servant killed it and then cut off its ears. He took the ears home with him and woke the prince.

"Take these to the king. Tell him you killed the dragon. He'll give you half his kingdom and his daughter in marriage," the servant said.

"But I didn't kill the dragon. You did. The reward should be yours," the prince said.

"Never mind that. Just do as I say, and everything will go well for you."

The prince did as his servant suggested. He brought the ears to the king, who immediately gave him half his kingdom and his daughter in marriage.

The prince and his wife soon had a fine son, and when the old king passed away, the prince was made ruler over the whole island.

One day, the servant went to the prince and said, "Sir, we should make another journey. Abdicate your throne in favor of your son. Make your wife regent. She is wise and will rule well. Then we sail for the Kingdom of the West. More good fortune awaits you there."

The prince did as his servant said, reluctantly saying farewell to his wife and child.

The two men set sail, and after a few days at sea, they arrived at the Kingdom of the West.

"Go to the palace and ask the king for his daughter's hand in marriage. She is the most beautiful woman in the world and will make you a fine wife," the servant told the prince.

The prince duly went to the palace and asked for an audience with the king.

When the king heard that the prince wanted to wed his daughter, he said, "You seem like a fine young man, and I'm sure you'd make a good husband for my daughter. But you should know that I have already tried ninety-nine times to wed my daughter, and every time, the poor young man dies on the wedding night. You can marry her as well if you like, but don't say I didn't warn you."

At first, the prince balked at marrying the king's daughter, but the servant reassured him.

"Never fear. It will all go well in the end. I'll see to that," he said.

The next day, the prince and princess were wed in a sumptuous ceremony. When the wedding feast was done, the young couple retired to their chamber. The prince was horrified to see that a coffin and a shroud had already been prepared and were waiting at the foot of the bed.

"What is this for?" the prince asked his bride.

"I'm sure my father told you the story. Some time ago, they decided to keep one of those in my chamber to save the trouble of making one on the morning after my weddings. I know it's strange, but you did know the danger when you agreed to marry me," the princess replied.

The young people went to bed and soon were asleep.

Now, during the wedding banquet, the servant had excused himself, saying that he wanted to be sure everything was ready in the bridal chamber, but what he really wanted to do was find a place to hide. He armed himself with a pair of tongs and a sharp dagger and then secreted himself into a wardrobe and waited until the prince and his bride were asleep. The servant eased the wardrobe door open and crept to the edge of the bed. The princess opened her mouth in her sleep, and what should come slithering out but a long, black viper! The servant grabbed the viper with the tongs and sliced off its head. He took the weapons and the serpent's body and buried them in the castle gardens.

In the morning, some men came into the bedchamber. The king had sent them to deal with the prince's dead body, but when they entered the room, they found that the prince was quite alive, sitting in bed and chatting with his wife over a breakfast prepared by the prince's servant. The king was overjoyed to see that the groom had lived out his wedding night.

"This marriage surely will be blessed. My daughter finally has a husband who can love her for all her days," he said.

The prince and his bride lived happily in the palace for a time, but soon the old king died. Since the king had no male heir, the prince took his throne. He ruled the kingdom well for some years until, one day, a messenger came to his court.

"I have been sent by your royal mother. Your father is dead. You've inherited his kingdom. Please come home at once," the messenger said.

The prince found a regent to rule in his stead and then took ship with his wife.

On the way, they stopped at the island to fetch the prince's first wife and his son. Then they sailed for his father's kingdom. They were welcomed with great rejoicing, and soon the prince and his family had made their home in the palace. Thus, the prince became lord not only over his father's kingdom but also of the island and the Kingdom of the West.

One day, the servant came to the prince and said, "Sir, you have two beautiful wives, a goodly kingdom, and vast treasure. My time with you is done. I must return to my home."

The prince was saddened to hear this. "Can't I persuade you to stay? You have advised me and served me well, and I am very grateful."

"No. I really must go."

"Very well, but take any amount of my treasure with you. All I have is yours, for I would have none of it at all if it weren't for you. You saved my life."

"I require no treasure, for I was only repaying my debt to you. You see, I am the golden-headed fish."

Part II: National Epics

David of Sassoun (*Armenia*)

"David of Sassoun" is the Armenian national epic. It covers the history of four generations of the same family, starting with the twin brothers Sanasar and Baghdasar, who are miraculously conceived when their mother drinks water from a magic spring. Like many heroes conceived by magic or miracle, Sanasar and Baghdasar are larger than life, have superhuman strength, and own a supernatural and immortal horse named Kourkig Jelaly ("Majestic Horse"). Many of the brothers' qualities are passed down from generation to generation, including to their grandson David, the eponymous hero of the epic. The story is set in Sassoun, which today is the district of Sason in the Batman Province of Southeastern Turkey—although historically, this area was Armenian territory, and according to the epic, was founded by Sanasar and Baghdasar themselves.

One focus of this story is the conflict between the Christian Armenians and their Muslim occupiers, reflecting historical truth. In the seventh century, Armenia was a province of the Umayyad Caliphate, and in the eleventh century, Armenia was invaded by the Muslim Seljuk Turks. The epic itself opens on a scene of conflict between Armenians and invading Muslims, in which the king of Armenia is forced to give his daughter, Dzovinar, to the Muslim

Caliph as part of a peace treaty. When Dzovinar conceives Sanasar and Baghasar, the Caliph is furious and plots to kill Dzovinar and her children. The boys evade execution and eventually rescue their mother from the Caliph's clutches, and so begins the tale of their dynasty.

We also see how Persian culture intermingled with Armenia in the characters of the devs, evil demon-like beings who steal some of David's cattle. Devs originally were creatures from Persian mythology but were eventually adopted into the mythologies of surrounding nations, including Armenia.

Because the entire epic is too long for this present volume, only a brief part is included here, and it has been rendered in prose rather than in its original poetic form. We join the story after the death of Sanasar's son, Medz ("Lion") Mher. Mher's wife then dies of grief, leaving their young son, David, an orphan. The crosscurrents between Armenians and their Muslim occupiers continue in this part of the epic, with the conflict between David and the Arab Msrah Melik, whose name means "king of Msr." Most translators render Msr as "Egypt," but in his translation of the epic, Artin Shalian says that "Msr" actually refers to a place in ancient Assyria.

David the Herdsman

When David was but a lad, he got into trouble so often that the townspeople begged his uncle Ohan to give him some occupation.

Ohan went to the boy and said, "Dear David, how would you like to herd the people's sheep and goats?"

"Yes, I think I'd like that. How do I do it?" David replied.

"You take the animals up to the pasture in the morning and drive them back home in the evening."

"Very well, but I'll need new shoes."

Ohan went to the blacksmith and had him make a pair of steel boots and an iron crook for him to use in herding the sheep. David was very pleased with his boots and crook and couldn't wait for morning to come so that he could start his work.

Finally, the new day dawned. David went to all his neighbors and offered to take their flocks out to pasture. The people all agreed, and soon David was in charge of a great flock of sheep and goats. He herded them up into the hills so that they could graze. When it came time to take the animals back home, he noticed that they were scattered about the hills.

What shall I do? I have to bring them all back, David thought.

David immediately went to work rounding up all the sheep and the goats, but in his enthusiasm, he also rounded up martens and ermines, pheasants and rabbits, and even a few foxes and placed them among the animals belonging to his neighbors. When the people of Sassoun saw David returning not only with goats and sheep but a great number of wild animals, they became afraid and hid in their homes.

"What have you done?" Ohan asked when he saw the motley herd David was driving through the town.

"I gathered up all the beasts and am bringing them home. I even found a few more to add to the flock," David replied.

"Yes, but only some of those are sheep and goats. The rest are wild animals."

Then Ohan had to show David how to tell the sheep and goats from the other creatures, and when the people stopped being afraid, they took the martens and ermines and foxes and used their skins to make fine furs for the winter, and they ate the pheasants and rabbits for their dinners.

The next day, the people went to Ohan and said, "Your nephew didn't exactly cause a disaster yesterday, but we don't want him herding our flocks anymore. Give him something else to do."

Ohan said to his nephew, "The people don't want you herding their sheep and goats anymore. How about you take the cattle up to the pasture instead?"

"Yes, I'll do that, Uncle, but I need a new pair of shoes. I already wore out the ones you gave me the other day," David replied.

So, Ohan had the blacksmith make David another pair of steel boots, and in the morning, David collected the cattle and brought them up to the pasture. This time, though, his uncle made sure to tell him only to bring back the animals he was taking up in the morning and to take nothing that looked different from the animals in his herd. David soon learned to herd the cattle well, and they prospered under his care. David also made friends with other herdsmen, and they watched their animals together.

One day, David and his friends were taking the cattle out to pasture as usual when David saw many people going toward the church.

"Where are they going?" David asked.

"It's a holy day today. They're going to church, and then afterward, they will eat and celebrate," one of the herdsmen replied.

Another herdsman said, "I wish I could eat and celebrate, too. That stew they make for the festival, it's so good!"

"If you watch my cattle, I'll go and get some stew for all of us," David said.

The herdsmen agreed, and so David set off for the church.

At the church, David found the women preparing several cauldrons of delicious-smelling stew.

"Greetings. May I have some stew to take back to my friends? We are herding everyone's cattle, and so can't come to the celebration," David said.

"No, you certainly may not have any stew," one of the women replied.

"But my friends and I are hungry, and I see here that you have plenty."

"Even so, you may not have any."

"We'll see about that."

David took his oaken staff and thrust it through the rings of one of the cauldrons. Then he picked up the cauldron, using the staff for a handle. He grabbed a few loaves of bread from a nearby table and started walking back to where his friends were waiting.

"Now, wait just one minute! Come back with our stew!" one of the women cried.

Just then, the priest came out of the church. He saw David walking off, carrying the enormous cauldron full of stew with only one hand.

"Hush, Mother. Don't you see that he's one of those men from Sassoun? That he's Medz Mher's son? Don't make him angry, or he'll come back and kill us all. We still have plenty for everyone else. Let it be," the priest said.

David strode back to the pasture, where he found his friends standing uneasily in a group.

David put down the cauldron and said, "Hey, boys, come and eat! Doesn't this smell good? I brought us some bread, too." When the other men didn't move or say anything, David added, "What's gotten into you? I went all the way to the church to get this, and now you won't eat it?"

"It's not that, David. It's that while you were gone, forty terrible devs came and drove off our cattle," one of the herdsmen said.

"Did they, now? Well, I'll not tend to forty devs on an empty stomach. Come on, let's eat, and then I'll go get our cattle back."

After David and the herdsmen had eaten their fill, David said, "Tell me which way the devs went."

The herdsmen showed him, and so David followed the tracks of the cattle up into the mountains. The tracks went into a cave from which smoke was issuing. David peered inside the cave, and there were the forty terrible devs. The devs had already slaughtered the cattle, skinned them, and put the meat on to boil in a huge cauldron. When he saw this, David was enraged. He roared a roar so loud that all the devs were quaking.

"That was Medz Mher's son for sure. Quick, go and pacify him before he kills us all," the chief of the devs said.

The devs went to speak with David, but he beheaded them with his staff one by one until none were left alive. Then David went into the cave, where he found the kettle full of meat, a pile of hides, and a great mountain of treasure. There was also a great stallion tied to a ring in one wall. David dumped the meat out of the kettle and filled it with treasure. Then he picked up the hides and the kettle full of treasure and went back to the village, where he distributed the wealth and arranged for the cattle owners to give the hides to those who needed them most. The kettle he gave to the women at the church, in exchange for the one he had taken earlier.

David went home to fetch his uncle and tell him about the treasure.

"Bring some asses to carry the loot. Even I can't carry all that by myself," David said.

David and his uncle went up to the cave. When the uncle saw the devs' headless bodies, he went nearly as white as snow and started to run away.

"Why are you running? They're dead. They won't harm anyone anymore," David said.

The two men went into the cave.

When Ohan saw the treasure and the horse, he said, "Oh! This is Medz Mher's treasure and his horse! The devs have been stealing this since he died."

"I'll give you all the treasure if you give me the horse. And I warn you to do as I ask, or I will have to hurt you," David said.

"The treasure and the horse all belong to you. I don't want any of it."

"I have no use for the treasure. Bring it home and give it to everyone in the town. I only want the horse."

And so, Sassoun became very wealthy, and all the people were happy.

David Rebuilds His Father's Monastery

One day, not long after he defeated the devs, David bought a hunting falcon and then rode his horse out to see whether his falcon might catch any birds for him. David was intent on his hunt, so he didn't pay attention to where he was riding. He ended up in a millet field, and his horse's hooves churned all the furrows to mud and crushed the young shoots of millet.

The old woman who owned the field came hobbling out of her house and shouted at David. "You there! What do you think you're doing, trampling my fine millet? If you want to hunt, go up into the mountains, to your father's old hunting place. There are good, fat sheep up there. After all, what kind of a meal will a sparrow make? Put away your falcon. Get a bow and some arrows, and go hunt sheep."

David went home and stood before his uncle. "Uncle, why did you never tell me that my father had hunting grounds in the mountains? You must give me a bow and some arrows and take me to the hunting place."

"Who told you about that hunting ground?" Ohan said.

"Never mind about that. Tell me where it is, and give me a bow and some arrows."

"We don't have the hunting ground anymore. When Msrah Melik and his armies came, they took it over. We don't dare go up there for fear of Melik's wrath."

David scoffed. "Melik's wrath means nothing to me. Now, get me a bow and some arrows, and get your own hunting gear. We're going up there to see what that place is like now."

Ohan protested some more, refusing to take David and refusing to give him a bow.

Finally, David said, "If you don't do as I say, I will hurt you."

At that, Ohan gave in. He went into another room and brought out a mighty bow and a quiver of arrows. "This was your father's bow, the bow of Medz Mher. No one has used it since he died because no one has been strong enough to string it. Maybe you are strong enough."

David took the bow and strung it easily. He strapped the bow and quiver to his back. "Now fetch your bow and quiver. We're leaving."

David followed his uncle up into the mountains. Soon they came across a place that once had been enclosed by a wall, but now the wall was a crumbling ruin, and the forest beyond was overgrown and ill-kept. Not one bit of game was in sight.

"What is this place?" David asked.

"This, lad, is your father's game preserve, or what is left of it since Melik took it for himself," Ohan replied.

David and his uncle spent the rest of the day exploring the abandoned reserve. When it began to get dark, they found a place to set up their camp. Ohan lay down and went to sleep immediately, but David was restless. He sat beside his snoring uncle as the light faded from the sky, wondering what he would do about his father's game preserve.

After some hours, a flickering light in the distance caught David's eye.

I wonder what that is, David thought, and without waking his uncle, he began to climb up the mountainside toward the light.

When he got to the top of the mountain, he found a slab of white marble that had been cleft in two, and from the cleft, a flame leaped up. David raced back down the mountain and roused his uncle.

"Uncle! Uncle! Wake up! There's something you need to see!" David said.

Ohan sat up, blinking blearily. "What is it that is so important that you rouse an old man from his sleep in the middle of the night?"

"Look!" David pointed up the mountain slope to where the light still flickered and danced. "I already went up there and found a marble slab that was cleft in two and a flame burning from out of the cleft."

"Ah. Yes, I know what that is. The marble slab is all that is left of the altar of the monastery that your father built, the monastery of Our Lady of Marout. Your father's tomb was in the monastery, but I expect that was damaged as well when Melik and his army invaded Sassoun. They wrecked the monastery just like they wrecked the game preserve."

"Oh, Uncle, we must rebuild it right away. We have to rebuild this monastery. Go into the town and gather up all the stonemasons and carpenters and workmen you can find. Send them here now so that we can rebuild this holy place. I will wait for you here. And when the monastery is rebuilt, you will go and gather monks and priests and bishops so that they can live here and worship God as they ought to do, and the people of Sassoun will have this holy place restored as my father would have wished it to be."

Ohan knew better than to argue when David was in this sort of mood, so he immediately set off down the mountainside and into the town. He told all the people that David intended to restore the monastery, and soon every artisan and builder and worker in stone and wood from miles around hastened up the mountain to help with the work.

Everyone worked as hard as they could and as quickly as they could, and soon the monastery was restored to its former state and peopled with holy men to sing Mass and say the other prayers they were wont to offer throughout the day. Not until the monastery was rebuilt and peopled with monks did David descend from the mountain peak.

It didn't take long for Msrah Melik to hear that the monastery had been rebuilt. "It's that infidel David who's behind this I'll wager. And I have just recalled that I've not had tribute from Sassoun for seven years now. It's high time my army paid them a visit and put them in their place."

Melik summoned the generals of his army. Their leader was a man named Gospadin.

Melik said to Gospadin, "Gather your men. Go to Sassoun. Collect up all the treasure they owe me, seven years' worth, and bring me the best of their women. We could use some more slaves. And when you're done collecting everything, raze Sassoun to the ground. Then kill that rogue David, and bring me his head."

"I will do this, but I expect to be well paid for it," Gospadin said.

"Never fear. If you manage all of that, you can have half my kingdom."

Gospadin mustered a thousand soldiers and placed his most trusted lieutenants in positions of command. Then they marched on Sassoun, relishing the thought that soon they would be wealthy and their enemy's country razed to the ground.

Gospadin and his men made their camp and sent a messenger into the town.

The messenger went to Ohan and said, "Msrah Melik has sent his army to collect the tribute you owe him, seven years' worth, and the best of your women. Gospadin, the general of the army, is on his way now. If you do not pay, the army will slaughter every last one of you and take everything anyway."

Ohan paled at the words of the messenger. "We will pay, never fear."

As soon as the messenger had gone, Ohan went in search of his nephew.

"David, my lad, it's been too long since we've eaten any game. How about you go up the mountainside and see whether you can catch a fine sheep for our dinner?" Ohan did this because he was ashamed of paying tribute to Melik and didn't want David to know about it.

David took his bow and quiver and went hunting. Not long afterward, Gospadin and his army arrived at the gates of Sassoun. The soldiers went throughout the city and the farmsteads around. They took all the cattle and goats and sheep and put them in a holding pen together. Then they chose the best of the women and locked them in a barn to wait while they collected the rest of the tribute.

Meanwhile, David was hunting in the mountains. He soon came across a fine, fat sheep, and when he had killed it, he hoisted it onto his shoulders and set off for home. On the way, he stopped at the farm owned by the old woman and pulled up a turnip to munch on his way home. When David arrived at the town, he saw the people in mourning.

The old woman caught sight of David, and with tears streaming down her cheeks, she said, "So this is what the champion of Sassoun does when our enemies come to call: He goes to my turnip field and helps himself while Msrah Melik's soldiers take everything we own. Those soldiers even took my daughter, curse you! My only daughter! And you stand by like nothing has happened at all! They've taken all the cattle, sheep, and goats, and now they're sitting in the treasure house counting out your father's gold to take back to that monster, Melik!"

"I was away hunting, Old One. Show me where they took your daughter. I will help her," David said.

The old woman showed David the barn where the women were being held. David broke down the door and set the women free. Next, David went to the place where Melik's soldiers were keeping the herds and flocks and set the animals free.

"Now, Old One, show me where they're counting out the gold," David said.

The old woman pointed to the treasure house. Outside the door, forty soldiers were standing guard.

With the sheep he had killed in the mountains slung over his shoulder, David strode up to the guards and said, "I heard that my uncle is in there and that he needs my help."

"Did you now? Well, I expect that someone was playing tricks on you. Go home, boy. You're not wanted here," the chief of the guards said.

At that, David put down the sheep and attacked the guards. He wrung the necks of every last one of them and left their bodies piled up just outside the door. Then David picked up the sheep again and went into the treasure house, where he saw his Uncle Ohan and his Uncle Vergo counting out treasure and putting it into sacks while Msrah Melik's generals looked on. Ohan was holding the sack open while Vergo scooped up gold with a bucket and poured it in. They had already filled several sacks, which had been lined up against one wall.

"Uncle Ohan! Uncle Vergo!" David said as he put down the sheep's carcass. "You really shouldn't be doing that. That's work for younger men. Let me help you."

"Get rid of this brat. Get him out of here and get on with your work," Gospadin told Ohan.

"No, I will stay and help. It is my duty to help my elders," David said.

"Go away, David. We don't want any trouble. Vergo and I can do this ourselves," Ohan told his nephew.

"No, I think I'll stay and help." David took the bucket from his uncle and held it upside down. "Now, Uncle, a measure of gold for Msrah Melik."

Ohan put a shovelful of gold onto the bottom of the upturned bucket. Then David went over to the sack, shook the gold off the bucket and onto the floor, and then pretended to empty the bucket into the sack.

"There! One scoop of treasure. See how helpful I can be?" David said.

"Get out! Get out before I slice off that fool head of yours and set the entire town ablaze!" Gospadin shouted.

In response, David hurled the bucket at Gospadin. If Gospadin hadn't ducked just in time, the bucket surely would have killed him. Gospadin became frightened and tried to run away, but David caught him, cut off his lips, pulled out his teeth, and lodged the teeth in his forehead.

Then David tied Gospadin to a horse and said, "Go back to Msrah Melik and tell him that the son of Medz Mher did this. Also tell Melik that what happened to you will happen to him if he ever tries to take tribute from us again. Our treasure, cattle, and women don't belong to him. Let him have Msr, and let us have Sassoun. But if he won't be satisfied with what he already has, let him come here so that I can deal with him."

Gospadin and the other generals raced back to their country, leaving their troops behind. But the soldiers didn't mind; they had set off on their own way to enjoy the treasure, women, and slaves they had looted from the town. It didn't take long for David to catch up to the soldiers of Msrah Melik.

"Hey, there! You're taking things that don't belong to you. That's not a very nice thing to do. Give it all back, or something bad will happen to you," David said.

The soldiers laughed. "Yes, and what are you going to do about it if we don't give it back? We're a whole army here, and you are only one man."

At that, David took his spear and fell upon the soldiers of Msrah Melik. He didn't stop fighting until he had killed every last one of them.

Then David set all the captives free and said, "Help me bring all this treasure back home so that we can give it back to whoever owns it."

The captives helped David bring everything back to Sassoun, where David ensured that the captives were returned safely to their families and every bit of treasure went only to the person it belonged to.

David's Battle with Msrah Melik

When Gospadin and the other generals returned to Msr, they were so ashamed that they hid. It wasn't until Melik asked whether his army had returned with the tribute that someone told him what had happened. Melik then summoned Gospadin to account for himself. When Gospodin arrived, Melik saw the wounds that David had inflicted upon him.

"Whatever happened to you?" Melik asked, astonished at Gospadin's appearance. "And where is the treasure? Where are the cattle and the sheep and the women?"

Gospadin fell on his face before his king. "O mighty one, long may you reign. Did you not see what happened to my face? David did this, Medz Mher's whelp. I don't know what happened to my soldiers. They went their way, and I went mine. And David has a message for you."

"Indeed. Tell it to me."

"David says that if you're not satisfied with having your own country but want his as well, you need to go to Sassoun so that he can deal with you."

When Melik heard this, he fell into a rage. "Assemble my army! Every male able to bear arms is to come here at once! I don't care how young or old, give each one a shirt of mail, a helmet, and a sword and tell him that we march on Sassoun tomorrow!"

Now, Ohan was in great fright after David sent Gospadin and the other generals running back home and after he had killed all of Melik's soldiers. Ohan knew it was only a matter of time before Melik assembled another, larger army and marched straight to Sassoun, and this time, no amount of treasure would keep him from killing everyone and burning down their homes.

So, one day, as Ohan made the rounds that he had appointed for himself—to watch for Melik's army— he saw a great host of tents had been erected on the plain not far from the town. Ohan ran back home as fast as he could and called for his nephew.

"What is it, Uncle? What frightens you so?" David asked.

"I told you! I told you your actions would be our doom! Even now, Melik's host is camped on our doorstep. There are too many tents to count. It looks like snow has fallen on the plain. There are so many white tents so close together. We are doomed. We should gather our women and our treasure and fly, right now, or we are all dead!" Ohan said.

"Never fear, Uncle. I'll keep us all safe."

David rushed over to the home of the old woman who was his friend.

"Old One, I need your help. Have you an old poker or skewer or something I can have? And can I borrow your donkey?"

"Whatever for?" the old woman asked.

"Msrah Melik has arrived with his army. They've covered the plain with their tents. I'm going to make war on them."

"Make war? The very son of Medz Mher will go to war astride a donkey with a rusty old skewer in one hand? Over my dead body, you are. Listen to me, you young fool. Your father had the best weapons in the world. He had the Lightning Sword. He had a mail shirt so tough that no weapon could pierce it and a shining helmet to go with it. He had the fiercest, fastest steed in the whole world, Kourkig Jelaly himself. You need to get those things if you want to fight Melik and the host of Msr properly, as befits the son of Medz Mher."

"Tell me where I can find them, then."

"Oh, no, that I'll not do. Your uncle put a curse on anyone who tells where those things are hidden. No, if you want to find them, you'll have to pry that information out of Ohan."

David ran home. He grabbed his uncle by the shirt and lifted him off the ground. "Tell me where I can find my father's weapons and my father's horse. Tell me now, or I'll break your neck right here."

"Put me down, and I'll bring them to you, and a curse on the one who told you this," Ohan said.

David put Ohan down. Ohan went to the place where the weapons and the horse were kept and brought them back to David. David put on the mail shirt, helmet and strapped on his father's sword. He saddled and bridled the horse and mounted it. When Ohan saw David thus arrayed for battle, he began to weep.

"Oh, alas! Alas for the mail shirt and helmet! Alas for the Lightning Sword! Alas for Kourkig Jelaly!" he cried.

When David heard this, he became very angry. He was about to get off the horse and shout at his uncle when Ohan said, "Alas for David! Alas for the champion of Sassoun! Alas for the son of Medz Mher!"

Hearing his uncle's lament, David dismounted. He took his uncle's hand in his and gently kissed it. "Don't weep for me, Uncle. You have been a father to me, and I am grateful. But don't weep. I'll be home soon. You'll see."

David rode through the town dressed in his father's armor and armed with his father's sword, riding his father's steed. All the people of Sassoun rejoiced to see their champion on his way to fight for them.

"It's like Mher himself has come back to save us!" they said and cheered and sang for David to the gates of the city.

Now, David had another uncle named Toros, a giant of a man who was his mother's brother. When Toros saw David riding out to war, he uprooted an elm tree and hoisted it onto his shoulder.

Toros went to the camp of Melik's army and shouted, "Hey, you there! You in the tents! Don't you know that you're in Sassoun and David, the son of Medz Mher, is on his way to fight you?"

Then he took the tree in both hands and swung it around so that it swept away twenty of the tents with the men still inside them.

"Hey there!" Toros shouted as he swung away with the tree. "Make way for David! Give the lad room to fight!"

David rode Kourkig Jelaly up onto a rise near the camp.

He shouted in a great voice at Melik's army. "Get up! Stand on your feet! I won't have it said that I killed you while you were abed. Put on your armor! Mount your horses! I am here to make war on Msrah Melik!"

Then David put spurs to Kourkig Jelaly and roared into Melik's camp. Up and down the camp, he rode, laying about him with his father's sword. David fought through the whole morning and past the noon hour, and not one of Melik's soldiers could stand against him.

Finally, one old man in Melik's army said, "Let me go and talk to David. Maybe I can put a stop to this slaughter."

The old man went to David and said, "Young one, I am here to talk, not fight. Will you hear me?"

"I will," David replied.

"Look about you, at all the men you have slaughtered. They are old and young. Some of them had wives at home, and some had children. All had parents and uncles and aunts, sisters and brothers, who now will be in mourning. You don't know any of the men you killed, and they don't know you. What harm has any of us done to you? We came here because Melik forced us to. He said that he would kill us if we did not put on the armor he gave us and take up a sword against Sassoun. If your quarrel is with Melik, why don't you take it to him and leave the rest of us alone?"

"Very well. Tell me where I can find Melik, and I will do as you ask."

"His tent is the big one in the middle of the camp. You can see smoke coming out of the hole at the top. But that's not the smoke of a fire. That's Melik's breath."

David spurred Kourkig Jelaly and rode to the center of the camp. He reined in his horse at the entrance to Melik's tent.

"Where is Msrah Melik? Where is he skulking, hiding away while his men fight and die for him?" he shouted.

The soldiers who stood guard outside Melik's tent replied, "Our king is within, but he is asleep. It is his custom to sleep for seven days at a time. He has only been asleep for three days. There are four yet left before he wakes."

David was astounded. "How is it that your king will lie here peacefully asleep and not fight alongside his men? Go and wake him, now, so that I can put him to sleep for good."

The soldiers went into Melik's tent. They slapped the bare feet of their king, but all he did was mutter about fleas and roll over, still dead asleep. They heated a plowshare on the fire and held the hot metal against their king's back. This time Melik muttered about mosquitos, but he also woke up enough to see David standing there at the entrance to the tent. Melik sent a great blast of breath at David, with force enough to knock over many strong men. When David did not even waver, Melik roused himself all the way. The two men locked eyes for a long moment, and as they did so, Melik felt the strength ebbing out of his body.

But wily Melik was not so easily defeated.

He sat up and said, "Welcome, David. Come and sit on that rug so that we can talk awhile."

Now, when on campaign, Melik had the habit of digging a deep pit inside his tent and covering the hole with a rug. He would lure his enemies into the tent, and when they fell through the hole, he would have it blocked up and leave his victims to rot. Melik had done the same here, so when David came into the tent and stepped onto the rug, he fell into the deep shaft that Melik had dug.

Melik looked over the lip of the pit and leered at David. "The son of Medz Mher, indeed. You shall trouble me no more, young cur. You have met your match in me and your doom."

Then Melik ordered the pit to be covered by a millstone so that David could not escape.

That night, David's Uncle Ohan tossed and turned in his sleep. Finally, his wife could stand it no longer.

"Quit thrashing about like an eel, or I'll send you to the barn to sleep in the loft," she said.

"I've been having bad dreams. I think our David is in trouble," Ohan told her.

"The only trouble here is the trouble you'll be in if you don't let me sleep."

"Curse you, woman. I'll let you sleep all right. See? I'm getting out of bed. I'm going to go and find out what happened to our David if it's the last thing I do."

"Good. You go look for that silly little beast, and in the meantime, I'll get some rest."

Ohan dressed and put on his mail shirt and girded on his sword. Then he went to the barn where his horses were stabled.

He slapped the white horse on the rump and asked it, "How fast can you get me to Melik's camp?"

"I can have you there by morning," the horse replied.

"What use is that? I'm trying to rescue that young fool David, not attend his funeral."

Ohan went and slapped the red horse on the rump and asked it, "How fast can you get me to Melik's camp?"

"I can get you there in an hour," the horse replied.

"An hour? An hour? That's how you repay me for all the fine barley I feed you?"

Ohan went and slapped the black horse on the rump and asked it, "How fast can you get me to Melik's camp?"

"If you saddle and mount me now, I'll have you there before you get your right leg over my back and into the stirrup," the horse replied.

Ohan saddled the black horse and put his left foot into the stirrup. He started to swing himself up into the saddle, but before he could find his seat, the black horse took off like a bolt of lightning, and by the time Ohan had sat down and put his right foot into the stirrup, they were already on the ridge overlooking Melik's camp.

Kourkig Jelaly saw Ohan arrive and galloped up to him, neighing. When Ohan saw David's horse, his heart fell.

Our David is dead for sure. Or if not dead, taken captive, he thought.

Now, Ohan had a nickname: Big Voice. He was called this because he could shout and roar louder than any man alive. Ohan knew that the only way to find David was to roar and that he would have to roar louder than he had ever roared before. Ohan took seven ox hides and strapped them around his body so that his ribs would not break when he roared.

When all was ready, he stood at the edge of the ridge facing the camp and shouted: "David, my David, if you can hear me, invoke Our Lady of Marout! Invoke the Holy Cross! Our Lord and Lady will give you the strength to come home to me!"

So loud was Ohan's roar that David heard it even at the bottom of the pit.

"That's my uncle!" he said, and his heart leaped. Then he said, "May Our Lady of Marout and the Holy Cross give me strength!"

Gathering himself up, he coiled like a spring and jumped. He jumped so hard that he smashed right through the millstone, and to this day, there are pieces of that stone that have yet to fall to earth.

Melik saw that David had escaped the pit. "David! How pleasant to see you again. Come, sit and talk with me a while."

"I'll not sit with you ever again, and I'll not talk. Get your weapons and meet me in fair combat. If you refuse, you'll just prove yourself a coward—as if you haven't already by the way you took me prisoner," David said.

"Very well, but I reserve the right to strike the first blow."

"All right. You can strike first. I'll meet you on the plain when you're ready."

Msrah Melik strapped on his armor, mounted his horse, and took up his lance. He rode out to the plain where he found David waiting for him.

"I get the first blow, remember?" Melik said.

"I remember. Get on with it," David replied.

Melik knew that he would need a lot of power behind his blow if he were going to win the contest, so he rode his horse all the way to Diarbarkir, and then turned around and thundered back to the place where David was standing. He charged forward and struck a blow so mighty that the people back in the town wondered whether there had been an earthquake, while in the camp, the dust was so thick that it was hard to make out the outlines of the nearest tents.

"Ha! That will be the end of that pesky David. I'm sure no one could have survived that," Melik said.

But then David said, "No, sorry, you're wrong. I'm still here," and as the dust cleared, Melik saw David standing there, unhurt.

Melik was astonished. "Oh, well, I guess I didn't get enough of a run-up, then. Can I have another go?"

"Very well."

This time, Melik rode all the way to Aleppo. He rode back to the plain so fast that the wind of his passing was like a hurricane, and when he struck David, the ground shook, and the thunder rumbled, and the lightning flashed.

"That had to have been the end of David," Melik said, who couldn't see more than a few feet in front of him for all the rain and dust his charge had stirred up.

"No, sorry, still here," David said when the dust began to clear. "Is it my turn now?"

"Not yet. Obviously, my run-up wasn't good enough that time either. Can I have one more try?"

"One more, and then I get to have a go."

This time, Melik rode all the way to Msr. He came roaring back with such force that when he struck David, a cloud of dust went up above the tops of the mountains and blotted out the sun for three whole days.

When the dust began to clear, Melik said, "There. I've finally gotten rid of David. Sassoun is mine."

"No, sorry, it's not. I'm still here, and I believe it's my turn now," David said.

When Melik heard David speak and saw him standing there unhurt, he felt as though his bones had turned to water. He ran back to his tent, dove into the pit he had dug, and commanded that the pit be covered with forty oxhides and the hides be covered with forty millstones.

But Melik could not hide from David. David mounted his horse, drew his sword, and set off toward the camp and Melik's tent. On the way, an old woman ran onto David's path and threw herself at the horse's feet.

"O David! Melik is my son. Don't kill him. Kill me instead!" the old woman cried.

"I will count this as my first blow, even though I forbear to strike," David told her.

Then he spurred his horse and again rode toward the camp.

He hadn't gone far when a young woman ran onto his path and threw herself at the horse's feet.

"O David! Melik is my brother. Don't kill him. Kill me instead!" the young woman cried.

"I will count this as my second blow, even though I forbear to strike. Now, stand aside, for I have but one blow remaining, and I must make sure it hits home," David told her.

David spurred his horse into a gallop. When they got closer to Melik's tent, they saw the forty millstones piled on top of the pit. Kourkig Jelaly made a mighty leap, and on the way back down, David struck a colossal blow with the Lightning Sword of Medz Mher. So violent was that stroke that it shattered all forty millstones, cut through the forty ox hides, and sliced Msrah Melik in half.

Kourkig Jelaly lightly touched down to earth, and David wheeled him around to see what had become of his foe.

A faint voice from the bottom of the pit said, "Sorry, I'm still here. I'm not dead yet."

David was astonished. It surely was impossible that anyone had survived such a blow. He went and peered over the edge of the pit. There he saw Msrah Melik standing tall.

"If you're really still alive, prove it. Move about a bit," David said.

Melik moved a little, and as he did so, his body fell into two halves, one half falling one way and the other half falling another. When Melik's soldiers saw this, they quaked with fear.

"Don't be afraid. My war with you is done. You are not to blame for this. You are farmers and fishermen, cobblers and carpenters, all forced to come here against your will. Go home to your families. Ply your trades. But if any of you dare come back here to threaten Sassoun, you will have me to deal with. Go home to your families. Live good lives. Be prosperous. And tell everyone in Msr what happens when tyrants threaten freeborn people," David told them.

The Knight in the Panther's Skin (*Georgia*)

"The Knight in the Panther's Skin" is an epic poem in quatrains by medieval Georgian poet Shota Rustaveli (c. 1160-after c. 1220), whose surname suggests that he was from Rustavi, a city in Southeastern Georgia. Rustaveli was Finance Minister under Queen Tamar (r. 1184-1213). His story of the trials of Tariel and Avtandil, the two knights around whom the story revolves, is considered to be the Georgian national epic; at one time, every Georgian bride was expected to have a copy of the book as part of her dowry and be able to recite portions for her husband.

The epic begins with a long prologue in which Rustaveli praises Queen Tamar (to whom he refers as "King Tamar") and sets out the philosophical underpinnings of the poem that is to follow. The story is a romance in the medieval sense of the term; it is an episodic tale of quests, knightly deeds, and romantic love. Rustaveli claims it to be his rendering of a Persian story; however, the model for Rustaveli's epic has yet to be found, assuming that such a model ever existed in the first place. That said, the knight in the panther's skin does bear some superficial resemblance to the Persian hero Rostam, in that he also wears the skin of a great cat, is nearly invincible in battle, and rides a horse as fast as lightning.

The retelling presented below has been both rendered into prose and abridged to fit this present volume. We join the story after the knight Avtandil and his liege lord, Rostevan, have encountered the strange warrior in the panther's skin. Rostevan becomes obsessed with finding the man, needing to reassure himself that the man was truly human and not a demonic apparition. When messengers sent throughout the land cannot find the man, Rostevan decides that he must have been an apparition and lets go of the matter. However, Rostevan's daughter, Tinatin, who has been made ruler of the land by her father and with whom Avtandil is deeply in love, is not convinced that her father has been completely cured of his obsession, nor does she believe that the man was an apparition. Tinatin, who returns Avtandil's affections, therefore sends Avtandil on a three-year quest to find the stranger in the panther's skin. Avtandil's journey starts with only a single quest, but by the end, it has seen him go through a series of adventures filled with danger, battles, romantic love, and knightly courtesy.

Avtandil Meets the Knight in the Panther's Skin

Avtandil searched and searched for the mysterious knight until only three months were left to find him. He had just made camp for the knight when a party of hunters approached.

"Help us! Our brother has been struck by a madman and is dying!" the hunters said.

The men told their story to Avtandil, whose heart leaped when he heard that the madman they spoke of was none other than the knight he was seeking.

"Hey, there he goes now!" one of the hunters cried.

There across the plain, Avtandil could see the knight in his panther's skin, cantering along on a jet-black horse.

"You may stay here in my camp and eat of the game I caught. My quest is to find that man, and now I must leave," Avtandil told the hunters.

Avtandil mounted his horse and raced after the man in the panther's skin. As he rode, he thought about how best to approach the man.

"He doesn't seem to like people asking questions, and he certainly demands a great deal of respect. Maybe I should hang back and watch him for a while and then decide what to do," he said to himself.

For two days, the stranger rode on, and for two days, Avtandil followed him. On the third day, they came to a cliff. In the cliff's face was the entrance to a cave, and a stream flowed out of the cave and burbled its way through beds of rushes and stands of trees. Here, Avtandil dismounted his horse. He climbed as high as he could into one of the trees, giving him a commanding view of the stream and forest. He watched the stranger ride by, only stopping when he reached the mouth of the cave. There he dismounted, and out of the cave came a lovely woman. The woman led the horse into the cave and took off its saddle and bridle. She helped the man remove his armor, and then both of them went into the cave together just as the sun set and night fell.

Avtandil remained watching in the tree all night long, still wondering how he might find a way to speak to the man. In the morning, the woman helped to saddle and bridle the horse and then helped the man put on his armor. The man and the woman embraced, and then the man mounted his horse and rode away, while the woman stayed behind, shedding many bitter tears.

The man in the panther's skin rode along the stream, retracing his path from the day before. On his way through the trees, he passed by the place where Avtandil had hidden. Avtandil was finally able to get a good look at the stranger and was struck by the man's beauty. Avtandil did not doubt that this man could wrestle a lion and come away the victor. At first, Avtandil thought to jump on his own horse and follow the man, but then he thought better of it.

I'll go to the cave and talk with the woman. Maybe she can tell me the strange knight's story, and maybe she can introduce us later, he thought.

Avtandil climbed down from the tree and led his horse to the mouth of the cave. No sooner had he arrived than the young woman came running out, obviously thinking that her knight had come back, but when she saw Avtandil, she turned and ran back into the cave in fright. Avtandil followed and grabbed her by the wrist.

The young woman struggled to get free, all the while crying out, "Tariel! Tariel!"

"Don't worry. I won't hurt you! I mean you no harm. I'm here to ask about the knight who just left. From what you said, I gather his name is Tariel. Can you tell me about him?" Avtandil said.

The woman stopped struggling. "I'll not tell you anything. That story is not for your ears, and even if you ask me a hundred times, I'll not speak a word of it to you."

"Please, you have no idea what I have gone through to find that man. I have to know who he is, and you have to tell me."

The woman continued to refuse, and Avtandil continued to ask, until finally, Avtandil lost all patience.

He grabbed the woman by the hair and set a knife to her throat. "Tell me who that man is, or I will kill you."

"Go ahead. You won't get his story from me while I live, and when I'm dead, I certainly won't tell you anything. I'd rather die than speak to you."

At this, Avtandil let the woman go. He sheathed his knife and sat down on a nearby stone, his eyes filled with tears.

Then he knelt before the woman and said, weeping, "I have treated you very ill and have no right to expect that you'll forgive me. But you should know that I have done everything I have done because of love. My beloved Tinatin sent me here to find out who that man is, and I would rather die than disappoint her."

The woman saw Avtandil's tears and said, "A lover's path is often cruel, and love can make a man do things he might not otherwise do. I do forgive you, but I still won't tell you the knight's story. That is for him alone to tell. At least, our names I can give you: I am Asmat, and he is Tariel. You may wait here until he returns. I'll explain to him your plight and your quest, and maybe he will tell you what you want to know."

Just then, they heard the sound of a horse's feet splashing through the stream.

"Quick, hide! It will take some time to convince him to speak with you, and no stranger who has demanded speech of him has yet lived to hear the answer," Asmat said.

Asmat showed Avtandil a place where he could hide and then went to greet Tariel. As before, she helped unsaddle the horse and take off its bridle, and then she helped the knight take off his armor. She led the knight into the cave and had him sit down on one of the panther's skins that lined the floor. Then she lit a fire and began to cook something for them to eat. The entire time, tears coursed down the knight's cheeks, and when the meal was ready, he took only a few bites before throwing himself down on the couch that lay nearby, still weeping.

"Tariel, my dearest one, it pains me to see you thus. Every day you come back, and every day, you shed bitter tears. I may not be able to cure your grief, but surely it would help to share it with a friend? What you need is a brother in arms, a fellow knight who understands you and who can help you," Asmat said.

"Asmat, dear Asmat, I know you speak true, but I doubt there is anyone in the world who could befriend me like that."

Asmat knelt next to Tariel. "If I could bring you such a man, would you promise not to hurt him?"

"Indeed, I would promise that if you could find me such a companion. But I expect my promise will go to waste. I think such a man is someone who only lives in dreams."

Asmat went to the place where Avtandil was hiding.

"Come. I think he will speak with you," she said and led Avtandil to Tariel. "Tariel, this is Avtandil. He is a knight like you, and I think he could be your friend."

Tariel sat up and looked at Avtandil, and his heart was instantly filled with love for the young knight. Likewise, Avtandil gazed upon Tariel and found that he loved him as well.

The two men embraced and shook hands, and when they had finished greeting one another, Tariel said, "Come, be seated next to the fire, and tell me your story."

"I am a knight from Arabia. My liege lord's daughter, Tinatin, is my beloved, and for her, I would die. Her father, my liege lord, and I saw you once when we were out hunting. My lord sent some men to summon you back to meet him, but you killed them all and ran away, so Tinatin has sent me on a quest to find you. She gave me three years. That span will be up in only a few months. I had despaired of finding you, but then I encountered some hunters. You had wounded one of them with your whip, and they pointed you out to me. I followed you here and spoke with Asmat. She bade me wait, and then brought me here to you."

"Ah, yes, I remember the day of which you spoke. I now rue having killed those men. I was so deep in my thoughts that I did not realize they were messengers and not soldiers sent to kill me. As for the men you met, they tried to lay hands on me for no good reason, and so I defended myself." Tariel sighed. "Alas for those who burn in the fires of love! Asmat spoke true when she said you would be a boon companion for me. You also are a knight, and you also have a beloved from whom you have been parted. I am glad you have come to me, for your friendship is a little balm for my grief."

"Tariel," Asmat said, who had been sitting nearby and listening to the men, "why don't you tell Avtandil your story? You've held it in your breast for so long. It might bring you some comfort to share it with a friend."

"As always, you are wise, dear Asmat—although I fear the telling might be the death of me, so painful is the wound I bear because of love. But you are right. I should tell Avtandil my tale," Tariel said.

"I am listening, and any aid I might give you is yours for the asking," Avtandil said.

The Knight Tells His Tale

"My father was a vassal to Parsadan, the King of India. So well-beloved was my father that when he got my mother with child, Parsadan asked whether he might foster me since he and his queen had not been able to have children of their own. My parents were honored, and accordingly, I was brought up as though I were an heir of the blood. I was given the best teaching, both for mind and body, and by the time I was five years old, I could wrestle a full-grown lion and take no hurt myself. But that fifth year also saw my undoing: The queen found herself with child, and when her time came, she delivered a daughter, who was named Nestan-Daredjan.

"There are no words to praise the beauty of Nestan-Daredjan. She was my childhood companion from the day of her birth until she reached her tenth year, and I my fifteenth. It was then that her father sent her away to be tutored, for she was now the heir to Parsadan's throne. I went back to live with my parents, and for a time, I was happy, while my beloved Nestan-Daredjan lived in a tower her father had built for her, learning everything she needed to know from Parsadan's widowed sister, and tended by dear Asmat here and one other maid.

"When my father died, Parsadan gave me his place at court. I now found myself lord of many lands and many vassals, and I tried to administer them as well as my father had. One day, Parsadan asked me to hunt some game birds and bring them to his daughter's tower. I did as he commanded. When I brought the birds to the tower, Asmat came down to take them from me, but as she did so, a curtain parted, and there I saw Nestan-Daredjan. From that moment forth, my heart was no longer my own, and I became weak with love. The king and queen fretted over me. No doctor could cure my malady, and I dared not speak my love for fear of being banished from court.

"After a time, I felt better and went about my duties and my leisure almost as usual, though my heart still burned for Nestan. Then one day, my dear Asmat came to me bearing a letter. It was from Nestan-Daredjan, and O blissful day, the letter declared that she also loved me! I wrote back, confessing my love to her, and so it was that we first spoke of our joy.

"We sent letters to one another, secretly, for many days. Then a time came when India made war with the Khatavians. I led Parsadan's army, and despite the treachery of the Khatavian king, we won the day and brought the king and many of his soldiers back to India as captives. Everyone rejoiced at my victory, and at the victory banquet, my heart nearly burst, for my beloved Nestan was there sitting beside me at the feast. We contrived to meet in person a few times after that, and both thought that our joy would soon be complete.

"Then one day, Parsadan and his queen called me and their other advisors to their council chamber. They told us they had been considering marriage for their daughter and wanted to hear our opinions. I could hardly breathe. Would I soon have my heart's desire? No, that was not to be, for they were thinking to marry her to the son of the king of Khvarazm. What could I do but agree? Soon the matter was settled, and the sun was made dark in my eyes.

"The next day, my beloved summoned me. She accused me of treachery, of conspiring to marry her to someone else. I told her that the decision had been made without me, and her anger cooled.

Then she said, 'If you love me, you will do something for me.'

'Anything,' I said.

'You will kill my bridegroom.'

I agreed to do it.

"When the wedding party arrived, they set up tents and pavilions outside the city. That night, I crept into the bridegroom's tent. I beheaded him and stuck his head on a pole. Then I fled, accompanied by my most loyal followers. Parsadan soon found out what I had done and sent a letter to me.

'Why did you bring such dishonor upon our house? If you had wanted our daughter for your own bride, you had but to ask.'

I wrote back saying that I no longer wanted his daughter and that although I was in exile because of the shame of my deed, in time, the throne of India would be mine, for who else did Parsadan have to succeed him?

"I took up residence in a fortress not far from the capital, chafing daily for news of my beloved. News I did not get until one day, I looked over the parapet and saw two travelers coming down the road. One I recognized as Asmat, but she was in a sorry state. Her hair was matted, her clothes were torn, and there was blood on her face. I rushed down to greet her and escort her to safety. When I asked her how our dear Nestan fared, she began to weep. She told me that

Nestan's aunt feared that Parsadan would blame her for the plot to kill the son of the king of Khvarazm. The aunt beat Asmat and Nestan and then summoned two demons carrying a chest between them. The demons seized Nestan, put her in the chest, locked it, and then ran away—who knows where? And no one has seen Nestan since, but for one man, and even he knows not where she is.

"Asmat and I went looking for Nestan. We searched for a year, but nowhere did we find her. For a time, we resided with Nureddin Pridon, the king of a far country. He was the man who once thought he had seen Nestan. We searched and searched, but we did not find her in Pridon's land, either. Our grief led us here, and we have lived in this cave ever since. Asmat stays here and tends the hearth while I roam the world, hunting for our food, insensible to man and beast alike, seeing nothing since my sun has been taken from me. Now you have heard all my tale, and now you should leave. Go back to your Tinatin. Lovers never should be parted."

Avtandil was silent for a time after Tariel finished his story, and when he spoke, his voice was thick with tears.

"My friend, I mourn with you for the loss of your dear Nestan. The burden you bear is so much heavier than mine. I think my back would have broken with it long since had I been in your place. But hear me: Perhaps I can bring an end to your grief. I will return to Tinatin, but I will not stay. I will beg leave to go look for your Nestan, and when I have found her, I will bring her to you, and you will have joy again."

"Dearest Avtandil," Tariel said, his tears bursting forth anew, "I bless the day when God sent you to us. Asmat said you would be a friend to me and a truer friend I could never ask for. Go with my blessing, and may someday you will return my sun to me. I hope that when that day comes, Nestan and Asmat and I may sit and feast with you and your Tinatin, and then our joy will be complete."

Avtandil Returns Home

The next day, Avtandil bid farewell to Tariel and Asmat and rode home. At Rostevan's court, he was received with music and dancing, and a great feast was prepared. At the feast, Avtandil was reunited with his beloved Tinatin, and everyone was happy.

When everyone had eaten and drunk their fill, Rostevan asked Avtandil to tell his story. Avtandil rose and told of all the adventures he had while seeking Tariel, and then he told the story of finding Tariel himself. Next, he told Tariel's story, and everyone wept when Avtandil spoke of Tariel's grief. Everyone praised Avtandil for his strength and courage, but Avtandil, still thinking of his friend's sadness, gave no answer.

After the feast, Tinatin summoned Avtandil to her private quarters. The lovers greeted one another with great joy, and then Tinatin showed Avtandil to a seat.

Tinatin then asked, "I mourn with you for Tariel's loss. Is there nothing we can do to assuage his sorrow?"

"Only one thing . . . The return of his dear Nestan-Daredjan. I told him I would go and seek her on his behalf. I promised him I would, and I need to keep my word."

"Yes, you must keep your word. I would expect nothing less from you, though my own heart will be darkened until the day you return."

Avtandil spent many days at Rostevan's court. He went hunting with the king and enjoyed banquet after banquet. Rostevan was deeply content that the knight he loved, like his own son, had returned to him. Avtandil saw this and realized that Rostevan was unlikely to grant him leave to seek Nestan, but he knew that he would go on that quest, whether he had leave or not.

After a few more days at court, Avtandil went to the king's vizier and said, "Wise One, I have a quest I must undertake. You heard me tell the story of Tariel's woe. I promised him that I would return and then go and seek his beloved. I need you to go to King Rostevan and ask his leave on my behalf."

"It's a fool who will undertake an errand he knows will get him killed, and that's exactly what Rostevan will do to me if I tell him you want to leave," the vizier said.

"Yes, that might happen, but it might not. Ask him, and I will reward you greatly."

The vizier accordingly went to Rostevan. "O most majestic of kings. I come to you with a request from the knight Avtandil. As you know, he found the knight Tariel, and he told us all of Tariel's grief. Avtandil, therefore, begs your majesty's leave to go on a quest to find the fair Nestan-Daredjan."

At this, Rostevan flew into a rage. "What? That ungrateful whelp goes away for three whole years, and when he finally comes back to the only home he's known, he wants to go away again? Of course I'll not grant him leave, and if I didn't know that he had sent you here to ask on his behalf, I'd slice your head off on the spot. Now get out of my sight!"

The trembling vizier returned to Avtandil and told him what Rostevan's reply had been. Avtandil rewarded the vizier richly, as he had promised. Avtandil then sat down and wrote a letter to Rostevan:

> *To the mighty Rostevan, King of All Araby, from his humble servant Avtandil, greetings. Fate and love both command me to do what they bid, and I pray that you will be able to forgive my disobedience. I promised my friend that I would help him find his beloved, and my love for my friend is such that I cannot bear to forsake him. I humbly beseech you that if this quest should end with my death, take all my treasure and distribute part of it to those most in*

need, and use the residue for the building of some noble works, like bridges or homes, from which all might benefit. I also beg of you to favor my loyal servant Shermadin, by whose hand you receive this letter. He is the wisest man I know besides yourself; take him into your service, and you will be blessed with his good counsel and faithful administration of all his duties. For yourself, I wish long life, prosperity, and victory in all your battles, and I remain, as ever, your humble servant

Avtandil

Avtandil gave the letter to Shermadin, with instructions to deliver it discreetly to Rostevan. Then Avtandil and Shermadin embraced, weeping many tears, for they knew they might never see one another again. Avtandil mounted his horse and rode quietly out of the gate and away from the palace.

When Rostevan heard that Avtandil had left, his grief was inconsolable.

"Avtandil was like a son to me. How shall I ever ride to the hunt again or feast at a banquet without him by my side?" he said.

He ordered the whole court to go into mourning, feeling betrayed that Avtandil had ridden away without saying farewell. Shermadin then deemed it safe to give Avtandil's letter to the king.

"Your royal majesty, I found this in my master Avtandil's chamber this morning. It is addressed to your majesty, and I expect it is his farewell to you."

Rostvan read the letter and wept more bitter tears, but his wounded heart was soothed somewhat, knowing that Avtandil had thought of him even as he was leaving disobediently.

"Let us all pray for brave Avtandil. Day and night, we will beseech the good God above to protect him, to bring his quest to a successful end, and bring him home safe to us," Rostevan said to his courtiers.

Avtandil Returns to Tariel and Asmat

Avtandil rode day and night toward the cave where Tariel and Asmat lived. When he arrived, Asmat came running out to greet him, but Avtandil could see that all was not well. Asmat looked pale and drawn, and she had been crying.

"O my sister, what has happened that you are so distraught?" Avtandil asked after they had embraced.

Asmat drew a shuddering breath. "Tariel is missing. He went out the day after you left us, and he has not been back since. I've searched for him myself, but how much can one woman do when she has not a mount to carry her?"

"Dear Asmat, have no fear. I'll look for him myself and bring him home safe. Have rugs and cushions laid and a fire burning, and wine in the cup ready for our return. I'll not be long. Keep in good heart!"

Avtandil mounted his horse and set off in the direction that Asmat had last seen Tariel go. He rode tirelessly throughout the day, his eyes always searching for his friend. The day had nearly ended when he spied Tariel's horse standing near a bed of reeds along a river. The horse's head was bowed down toward the ground, but Tariel himself was nowhere to be seen. Avtandil dismounted near Tariel's horse and went looking through the reeds. There, he found his friend, sitting near the riverbank.

"How now, dear friend. What are you doing here by yourself? Our sister Asmat mourns in your absence. Let us go home to her," Avtandil said.

Tariel didn't reply. He didn't even look up. Avtandil knelt beside him and saw that his friend was deathly pale, with sunken cheeks and matted hair, and tears were coursing down his face.

Avtandil gently wiped away Tariel's tears with his sleeve and said, "Tariel, it is I, Avtandil. I've returned as I said I would. Let's go home to Asmat. She is waiting for us."

Tariel spoke without looking at Avtandil. "Leave me alone. Leave me here and let me die. Death is all that is left for me now."

"Come now. Every lover suffers when his beloved is absent. My own heart is rent that I have had to part yet again from my dear Tinatin. What will Nestan-Daredjan do if she finds you have not the will to live, even for her? Mount your horse. Let's go home, where our sister Asmat waits for us."

Avtandil helped his friend rise and mount his horse, and together they rode back to the cave. Avtandil was pleased to see that Tariel seemed a little better for being on his horse, but he still was shocked and grieved by how ill Tariel seemed to be.

When they arrived at the cave, they found Asmat waiting for them. They dismounted, and the three friends embraced one another joyfully.

"I bless the day Avtandil became our friend, for without him, how would you have ever come home to me? Come inside, rest yourselves. We'll eat together and share our news," Asmat said.

The three went into the cave. Avtandil and Asmat helped Tariel sit on the panther's skin that Asmat always kept ready for him. Then Asmat cooked a meal, and the three talked of whatever pleased them. Asmat and Avtandil ate their fill, but Tariel barely took a bite.

When the meal was done, Tariel said, "Avtandil, my friend, it is clear that you are the most loyal of knights. You kept your promise to me and came back. But my grief is not yours to assuage. You should go back home to your beloved."

"That I'll not do. You are my brother, and I'll not see you wither away with grief. I promised to come back, and I promised to find your Nestan. How could I face my own beloved Tinatin, knowing that I turned my back on this quest? Be of good heart! Continue to live! I will go on this adventure, and if I have not returned by one year from today, you will know that I am dead, and then you may do with your life as you please," Avtandil said.

"Very well. I'll do as you ask. But I don't know what I'll do if, at the end of that year, I have neither you nor Nestan-Daredjan by my side."

In the morning, Avtandil bade farewell to Asmat.

"Come back to us soon. We need our brother here beside us," Asmat told Avtandil. Then she embraced Tariel and said, "Do not tarry. We will wait here together until Avtandil returns."

Tariel and Avtandil mounted their horses and rode away from the cave. Tariel went with Avtandil to show him what road to take to get to Pridon's land and because he was not yet ready to say farewell to his brother in arms. They rode all day, and when it came time for them to make their camp, they shot some game and roasted it over the fire.

In the morning, Tariel said, "Here we must part. Asmat awaits me. Take that road there eastward, and when you come to the seashore, ride along the beach until you come to Pridon's land. If he asks after me, you may tell him what you know."

Then the two friends embraced and said their farewells with many tears. Tariel mounted his horse and turned for home, while Avtandil mounted and rode eastward, as Tariel had told him to do.

Avtandil Visits Pridon

Avtandil rode until he came to the seashore. Then he turned his mount to ride along the coast. He traveled for seventy days, and on the seventieth day, he saw sails on the horizon. Since the ship was heading his way, Avtandil decided to wait and ask the sailors where he was and how much further he had to go.

Soon the little vessel was within shouting distance, so Avtandil called out, "Ahoy there! Can you tell me what land this is and who is its king?"

"You are standing on Turkish ground, but you are near the border with Pridon's land. Pridon is our king, the King of Mulghazanzar," the sailors replied.

"Good fortune is mine that I met you, for I ride in search of your king. Can you tell me how to find him?"

"Keep following the coastline. Two or three days' journey should bring you to the city where Pridon resides."

"Many thanks, friends, and may you always have calm seas and prosperous journeys!"

Avtandil rode on, following the coast as the sailors had told him to do. After two days, he came upon a line of men who had clearly been stationed to enclose something or someone in the field just above the beach. Avtandil spurred his horse to trot in their direction, and when he got closer, he saw that a hunting party was assembled in the field, shooting game with bows. A huge eagle flew above the party; Avtandil drew his bow and shot the eagle, which fell at the hunters' feet. The hunters turned to see who had made the shot and saw Avtandil there on his horse.

"A fine shot," one of the hunters said, but none of them dared stand in Avtandil's way; his nobility of bearing showed them that they should give him deference. Some of them even followed in his train.

On a knoll above the beach was a circle of soldiers surrounding a group of nobles, and among them was King Pridon. Pridon saw Avtandil approaching, with some of his men following along, and he said, "Go and see who that is, and find out why those men have left their stations."

The messenger ran to Avtandil and bowed before him. So stricken was he by Avtandil's beauty that he forgot what the king had told him to say.

Avtandil knew what the messenger's business was even without speech, so he said, "I am here to beg an audience of King Pridon. I am a friend to the knight Tariel, who also is known to your liege lord."

The messenger ran back to Pridon and delivered Avtandil's message. When Pridon heard Tariel's name spoken, he forgot his anger and went to greet Avtandil.

"Well met indeed. If you are a friend to Tariel, you are a friend to me. Come, ride with me to my palace, and on the way, pray tell me news of Tariel, for I have heard nothing for many a year," Pridon said.

"As your majesty pleases," Avtandil said.

All the way back to the palace, Avtandil rode beside Pridon and told him his tale—of his quest to find Tariel and how he and Tariel became brothers. Then he told Pridon of his quest to find Nestan-Daredjan. Pridon listened gladly, for he loved Tariel well and had longed to hear news of him. That night, Pridon caused a great banquet to be held in Avtandil's honor, and all who beheld the knight were awed by his beauty and courtesy. Although Avtandil was eager to resume his journey, he remained as Pridon's guest for some days, going hunting with his host and participating in the life of the court.

Finally, he went to Pridon and said, "Your majesty's gracious hospitality is matchless, but I find that I must resume my quest, for I promised Tariel I would look for Nestan-Daredjan and return within the year."

"Yes, I knew that you would soon depart, though it saddens me to see you leave. But I can't let you go without some gifts. I'll send some of my men along with you. I'll arm them well, and every last man will have a horse to ride. I'll also give you a mule to carry your provisions. I'll ride with you for a mile or two and show you the way you must go," Pridon said.

In the morning, Pridon summoned four of his best soldiers. He gave each of them new armor, new weapons, and a fierce warhorse to ride. He also gave new armor to Avtandil. The mule was duly laden with provisions, and when all was ready, Avtandil and Pridon rode out of the city together.

When they arrived at the seashore, they halted.

"This very spot is where I last saw Nestan-Daredjan. Two men were sailing her toward the shore in a small boat. It was clear to me that she was a prisoner. I drew my sword and tried to ride to her rescue, but when the men saw me, they turned their boat and fled. That was the last I saw of any of them," Pridon said.

Then Avtandil and Pridon said their farewells, and the king rode back to his court with a heavy heart, for he had come to love the young knight.

Avtandil and Patman

Avtandil and his companions rode along the seashore until they fell in with a company of merchants. They sailed with the merchants to the city of Gulansharo, and Avtandil earned the merchants' eternal friendship and praise by saving them from a band of pirates. Avtandil also decided that it might be best to disguise his true estate; if the jailers of Nestan-Daredjan were near, it would not do to let them know that a brave knight was on his way to rescue her. So, Avtandil and his companions dressed themselves like merchants and pretended to be part of the merchant band.

When the ship had been moored at the dock and the goods unloaded, Avtandil sat among the merchants, making bargains and taking orders from the servants who had been sent to buy goods for their employers. By and by, a man approached Avtandil.

Stricken by Avtandil's beauty, the man said, "Who are you and where are you from? I meet all the merchants who dock here, but I've never seen you before."

"I am a simple merchant, like all the others. But tell me of yourself. Who do you work for? What is this city? Who rules here? What do merchants customarily do when they arrive?" Avtandil replied.

"This is the city of Gulansharo. Melik Surkhavi, the King of the Sea, is our ruler. I am the gardener to Usen, the chief merchant of the city. Most merchants set aside the very best of their merchandise for Melik Surkhavi, but they first have to show that and everything else to Usen, and they have to give him gifts. Otherwise, he will ban them from trading. Would you like to meet him? I know his wife, Patman Khatun, is at home, and she always likes to meet new people. Also, you and your companions seem to have many costly wares. Usen and Patman will be grateful if you give them first pick."

Avtandil agreed that a visit to Usen and Patman would be worthwhile, so the gardener rushed home to make arrangements while Avtandil told his companions to get ready to go to their hosts' home.

When Patman heard that an exceedingly handsome merchant had arrived with costly wares, she sent ten servants to help Avtandil and his companions bring their things to the place where she lived, and while she waited for the merchants to arrive, she had her other servants set up tents for the merchants to dwell in and arranged for storage for their goods. Patman was waiting at the door for Avtandil and the other merchants. She made them very welcome while the servants tended to the pack animals and made sure the goods were all safely stored away.

In the morning, Avtandil had the merchants sent the best of their goods to the king, and after that, they began trading. Patman watched Avtandil all day and found that she desired him. She wrestled with her desire until finally, she wrote him a letter confessing her love. Avtandil received the letter and pondered what to do about it.

I do not return her affections, but she might be useful to me, and I could use her love as a lever to help find Nestan-Daredjan, he thought.

Therefore, Avtandil wrote back saying that he desired Patman in return and suggested that they meet in secret sometime soon.

After some days, Patman invited Avtandil to visit her in her chamber. Avtandil went, and they sat together on Patman's couch. Soon they progressed from sweet words to kissing, and while they were thus pleasantly engaged, a young knight burst into the room.

"And whatever is this, now?" the knight asked.

"Alas, I am undone! I am undone, and my husband and children with me!" Patman said.

"Yes, you are undone, and in the morning, I will kill your children and feed them to you, bite by bite." Then the knight left.

Patman lay weeping bitterly on her couch while Avtandil looked at her in confusion.

"Who was that man?" he asked.

"I can't tell you that. It would only make things worse. Suffice it to say that I am a woman and that I enjoy the company of men. But if you truly care about me, you'll kill that man before the night is over and bring me his ring as proof. I gave him that ring, so I'll know whether you're telling the truth," Patman replied.

"Very well, but I'll need a guide to the place where he lives."

Patman arranged for one of her servants to show Avtandil to the knight's house. When they arrived, they found the knight asleep on a couch on a terrace. Avtandil climbed silently up to the terrace, where he found two guards standing watch. He slew both before either could give the alarm. Then he went over to the young man and slit his throat. When the man was dead, Avtandil cut the ring off his finger and then tossed the body out the window and into the waves that lapped against the city's wall. Avtandil returned to Patman with the ring.

"He is dead. Here is his ring as proof. Now tell me: Who is that man, and what does he have against you? Why are you so afraid of him?" Avtandil said.

Patman's Tale

"You have saved me, and by doing so have saved my whole family. I owe you a debt, so I will tell you everything," Patman said.

"This started one night when I looked out my window and saw a small boat approaching. The boat was manned by two men, and the cargo was a large chest. When they had beached their boat, they picked up the chest, carried it up the beach, and opened it. Out of the chest stepped the most beautiful maiden I have ever seen. None can compare to her. I could see at once that the two men were brigands who had captured her. I sent some servants down to the beach to see whether they might purchase the woman's freedom. I told them that if the men refused to sell, kill them and bring the woman to me anyway.

"My servants went down to the beach while I watched from the window. For a little while, my servants haggled with the men, but when it became clear the men would never sell, I shouted, 'Kill them!' My servants beheaded the men and tossed their heads and bodies into the sea, then conducted the young woman to my house.

"I made the young woman very welcome. I asked her for her name and where she was from, and why the pirates had kidnapped her, but no matter how I asked or how often, she refused to answer. I gave her fresh clothes and put her in an apartment of my home with a servant to wait on her. I saw that she lacked for nothing. Every day I called on her to see how she was faring. Every day I asked her for her name and to tell me her tale, and every day, I got nothing but silence and tears in reply, though I could see by her clothing that she was of noble stock.

"Many days went by. I wondered how my husband would respond if he knew I was harboring this stranger. Finally, I decided that truth was better than deception, so I told Usen about the young woman. I made him promise never to tell anyone, and then I brought him to the woman's chamber. Usen was amazed by her beauty. We both sat with the woman for a while, asking her again who she was, but all she would do is weep. We wept with her—how could one not mourn with someone as beautiful and bereft as she? But even that would not soften her resolve.

"More time went by. Usen came to me and said, 'It's high time I visited the king and brought him gifts. He'll think me remiss if I don't go soon.'

"I replied, 'Very well, do as you must. But don't drink too much, and above all, don't mention our young guest to anyone!'

"Usen swore his lips were sealed, but, of course, as soon as he arrived at the banquet, he began drinking, and it didn't take long before he was in his cups. The king praised Usen for the jewels and pearls he had brought, and then Usen said, 'Aha, but I have one pearl yet that is greater than all of these,' and he told all about the young woman lodged in our home.

"The king, of course, demanded we bring our young guest to his court, and how could we refuse? I went to our guest's chamber and told her the unhappy news. 'Alas, it is my fate to be taken hither and thither. Never shall I have rest,' she said. Her grief smote my heart anew. I went to our treasure-room and chose the best jewels and pearls. I helped her hide them in her clothes. 'These may be useful to you sometime, and I'll not let a guest leave my home without a gift,' I said.

"We draped our guest in a veil, as is fitting, and brought her before the king. She received a fine welcome by his majesty and all the court, and for a time, none could speak but only gazed at her beauty. Finally, the king motioned for her to sit beside him. He asked her for her name and where she was from, but she remained steadfastly silent. Then the king thought that perhaps his son might be the one to assuage her grief. The crown prince is a good man, valiant and strong, and any woman would be proud to be his wife, but the news that the king sought to marry her to his son only refreshed the young woman's grief. Therefore, she conspired with the servants the king had given her. She gave them all her jewels and pearls, saying, 'These are yours if you help me escape.' The servants could not resist such a bribe.

They clothed the woman like a servant, whisked her out of the palace, and brought her to my door.

"'Servants helped me escape the palace, but now you must help me escape this city. Have you a swift horse that can carry me a far distance?' she said.

"I could not refuse her request. I gave her our best horse, and she rode it out of the city, unseen. I shall tell you what happened to her soon, but first, I must explain who that man was, of whom I was so afraid. He was a wine taster at the king's court, handsome and well made in his body. My husband is ugly and scrawny. I did a wife's duty to Usen, but I did not desire him, and after his treachery, I cannot bear even to look at him. The wine taster I desired, and he desired me. During one fateful night of pleasure, I told the wine taster that I had helped the young woman escape, and by this, he held me in thrall, knowing that I would be doomed should he but open his lips. You cannot know what a harsh fate you have delivered me from by killing that man!"

"Men such as that deserve death. I am glad your fear is eased. Now, tell me, what happened to the young woman after she departed your house?" Avtandil said.

"I fretted daily about my young friend, wondering whether she had found succor and safety. I heard nothing of her until one day, I sat by a window that overlooked the street, and across the street was an inn. Three wayfarers came to the inn, bought food and drink, and then sat outside to eat and enjoy one another's company. They began telling their tales to one another. I listened, thinking how merry it is to hear such things, when one of the wayfarers said, 'You've all told fine tales, but I'll wager you'll think mine the best. I used to be a slave to the king of the Kadjis. When he died, his sister Dulardukht took the throne because the royal children were too young to rule. A time came when Dulardukht's sister also died, so she left for the funeral. The foreman of the slaves, a man named Roshak, said, 'Now is our chance to escape and make our fortunes. Who will come with me?'

"'Of course, we all jumped at the chance to escape servitude and seek riches. We became bandits, harassing and looting caravans as often as we could. One night we were crossing a wide plain when in the distance, we saw a light. We wondered what it was, and when it drew close enough, we saw that it was a woman and that her beauty caused the radiance. We took her to Roshak, who asked her many questions, but no answer would she give except, 'Take me to Kadjeti. I have a message for the queen.' We agreed to take her. When we arrived at the border, I begged Roshak's leave to go to Gulansharo to do some business. He assented, and so here I am, and that's all my tale.'"

"I sent one of my servants to bring the wayfarer to me. I had him tell his tale over again, and when I was satisfied I had heard all, I paid him for his trouble and sent him away. Then I summoned two of my servants, sorcerers both. I sent them to Kadjeti to see what news they might gather of she who had been my guest. They learned that Dulardukht planned to marry the young woman to her nephew and that she was being kept in a tower at the center of the city, under constant guard. The tower is encircled by three walls, one within the other, and each wall is guarded by three thousand soldiers. I don't know how she will ever escape."

"Patman, I am grateful for your tale, but I beg to know one thing: I thought Kadjis were of demon-kind, not mortal people. How is it that human beings people Kadjeti?" Avtandil said.

"They are not true Kadjis but are called such because they are great sorcerers and command mighty magic."

Upon hearing all of Patman's tale, Avtandil's heart swelled with joy near to bursting. Now that he knew where Nestan-Daredjan was, he could tell Tariel that his beloved still lived, and together they could rescue her and bring her home to her knight.

Patman, for her part, rejoiced that her heart had been unburdened of its secrets, and so she and Avtandil passed the night together in pleasure, though Avtandil held no true love for Patman and thought only of his own beloved Tinatin.

The Rescue of Nestan-Daredjan

In the morning, Patman set a meal for the two of them while Avtandil changed his clothing.

It is time I revealed my true self to my hostess, he thought, and so he set aside his merchant's garb and dressed in a manner befitting a knight.

When Patman saw him, her breath was taken away. "That look is more befitting to you than the other."

Avtandil sat next to her and said gently, "Patman, I have not told you the truth about who I am. I am not a merchant. I am a vassal of King Rostevan. I command many men and own many lands. You have been the best of friends, and you cannot know how much that means to me. But you should also know that Rostevan has a daughter who is the sun in my sky. It is because of her that I am here, and my quest is to find that young woman who you aided and is so dear to you."

Then Avtandil told all of Tariel's tale to Patman, and when he was done, he said, "And so now you know the truth. Help me to find Nestan-Daredjan and bring her to safety, back to the man she loves and who loves her more than life itself. Send one of your sorcerers to Nestan. Let her know what we intend, and so bring her some solace."

"Anything within my power to do I will do for her, and for you," Patman said.

She then wrote a letter to Nestan, explaining who Avtandil was and what he intended to do, and gave it to one of her sorcerers. "Take this to the maid in the tower in Kadjeti. Do it secretly. If she wishes to send an answer, wait for her to write it, then bring it back to me right away."

The sorcerer hastened to Kadjeti and delivered Patman's message. Nestan was wary at first, but when the sorcerer had told all his tale, Nestan understood he was a friend. She wrote a letter to Patman in answer, and the sorcerer faithfully delivered it. Patman was overcome with joy when she received the letter and read it aloud so that Avtandil could hear:

Dearest Patman, to receive a letter from one who is like a mother to me is the greatest joy I have had in a long while. Even though the queen of the Kadjis and her chief sorcerers are still absent, the tower where I am imprisoned is nigh unassailable! Tell those bravest of the brave that they must not make the attempt, for I would die if they were slain; I can only live knowing that my sun still shines, albeit not for me. I here enclose a letter to my Tariel. Send with it this piece of the veil he gave me so that he will know that it is truly I who wrote it. Farewell.

When Avtandil heard Nestan-Daredjan's words, his heart was set aflame. "Patman, I must not tarry. I have to get this to Tariel and bring him back here before the queen of Kadjeti returns, for our task will be all the harder if we must face sorcerers in addition to soldiers."

"I know and understand, though my lover's heart quakes in fear for your safety. Go now and rescue the one beloved of me and your Tariel," Patman said.

Avtandil first penned a letter to Pridon, saying that Nestan-Daredjan had been found and he was going to fetch Tariel before attempting a rescue. He also asked for Pridon's aid, knowing that Pridon was a mighty warrior and had many fine soldiers at his command. He gave the letter to the servants Pridon had lent him and sent them back home with instructions to immediately give Pridon the letter.

It then was time for him to take his leave of Patman and her family. Many tears were shed, for Avtandil had become beloved of them all. Avtandil went down to the seaside and found a ship that would take him from Gulansharo to his own country by the swiftest route. When he disembarked, he rode as swiftly as he could to Tariel's cave.

First, I'll check by the river. Tariel likes to go there when he's sad. He's probably there rather than at home, Avtandil thought.

Avtandil was right; he found his friend standing amid the rushes near the river, a bloody sword in his hand, and next to him, the carcass of a lion he had slain. Avtandil jumped down from his horse and shouted a greeting to his friend. Tariel cried out with joy, and the two brothers ran to one another's arms. They embraced and kissed, delighted to see one another.

"Tariel, I have the best of news," Avtandil said.

"The best news is that you are here with me. Please don't tease me with false hopes."

"These hopes are not false. Look! I bear a letter to you, written by the hand of your beloved Nestan-Daredjan herself!"

Tariel took the letter and the scrap of veil with trembling hands. He pressed them to his lips, but when he inhaled the scent of his beloved's perfume, he fell to the ground, senseless.

"Oh, what have I done!" Avtandil cried.

He rushed to his friend's aid, but he could find neither a heartbeat nor a puff of breath. Avtandil called his friend's name, held his hand, but all to no avail. He went to the river to get some water but then thought of a better cure. He took some of the lion's blood and sprinkled it on his friend. Tariel took a breath again, and his pallor receded. He opened his eyes and found the strength to sit up. He opened Nestan's letter and read it, tears coursing down his cheeks all the while.

When he finished reading, he wiped his eyes and said, "Now is not the time for tears. It is the time for joy and laughter and knightly deeds. Come, let us go back home. We will tell Asmat the good news and arm ourselves for the coming battle. Avtandil, how can I ever repay you? The service you have rendered is worth more than my life itself. I have wept for so long, but you have dried my tears, and a new fire is rekindled in my breast."

The two friends mounted their horses and rode back to the cave, laughing and singing all the while. Asmat heard their voices and ran to greet her beloved brothers. Tears coursed down her cheeks, but these were tears of joy, not sorrow.

Tariel jumped down from his horse and ran to Asmat. "Asmat, dear Asmat! Our lives are renewed! Our brother has found our lost one!"

"Is it true? Nestan-Daredjan is found?" Asmat asked.

Avtandil alit from his horse and embraced Asmat. "It is true, dear sister! We have found her!" He showed Asmat Nestan's letter.

"Oh, this cannot be! This is not to be believed!" Asmat said.

"It is absolutely true."

Tariel then told Asmat how Nestan had been found. Tariel finished his tale, and then all three friends embraced once more.

"Come. Let's go and look at the treasure this cave holds. When I wrested it from the evil devs who lived here, I didn't care to count it, but perhaps there are things among the treasure that we might find useful in the task to come," Tariel said.

Asmat and Avtandil followed Tariel to a chamber deep within the cave. In that chamber was piled wealth immeasurable: Heaps of gold and silver as tall as a man, chests full of cut gems and pearls, embroidered silks encrusted with jewels, swords and spears, and three suits of armor, fit for a king, that no blade or bolt could pierce. Tariel and Avtandil put on some of the armor, setting aside the third suit to take to Pridon as a gift. They each took some gold and pearls, and then they sealed the treasure chamber up tight.

In the morning, the three friends started on their journey. They used some of their gold to buy a horse for Asmat, and together they rode to Pridon's country, with Avtandil as their guide. When they approached the border of Pridon's land, they saw a herd of horses with their guardian in a meadow.

"Let's play a trick on Pridon. Let's pretend to be rustlers, and when he comes storming out to see who is making off with his horses, he'll get a surprise!" Tariel said.

Avtandil and Tariel put on their armor and spurred their horses into Pridon's herd. Steed after steed, they roped and took away.

The herdsmen ran after them in vain, crying, "For shame! This is not a knightly deed, to behave as common thieves!"

One of the herdsmen set a great bonfire alight. When Pridon saw the signal fire, he armed himself and rode to the meadow with all speed. Now, Avtandil and Tariel had kept the visors of their helmets down; Pridon could not tell who they were by their dress.

Sword drawn, the king rode up to the two knights and said, "How now, what do you think you're doing with my horses?"

"Playing a trick on an old and very dear friend," Tariel replied as he lifted his visor and flashed a beaming smile at Pridon.

Then Avtandil did the same.

"God bless the two of you for knaves. And welcome, most welcome, dear friends! What took you so long? I expected your return some days ago. Come, let's go to my palace, and you can tell me all your tale. Any aid I can offer is yours for the asking," Pridon said.

Pridon had a meal set out for himself and his guests. He listened as Avtandil told him of his adventures and their plan to rescue Nestan. Then Tariel presented Pridon with the armor they had brought from the cave and the many jewels and pearls.

Pridon was overcome. "My dear friends, what have I done to deserve such largesse? Stay here and be my guests. Everything I have is yours."

Pridon had his guests conducted to fine chambers and had hot baths drawn and fresh clothing laid out for them. When Tariel and Avtandil were refreshed, they gathered with Pridon once again for a meal and to take counsel about what was to be done to free Nestan.

"If you take my advice, you'll not travel with a great host. No, three hundred of the best picked men will be more effective. We need speed if we are to get to Kadjeti before the queen and her sorcerers return," Pridon said.

Tariel and Avtandil agreed that this was the best path to follow. Pridon set preparations in motion, and in the morning, Pridon, Tariel, and Avtandil were armed and ready to ride with three hundred of Pridon's best soldiers, every man a hero. The three knights took their leave of Asmat and rode to the seashore, where they took ship to Gulansharo.

When they disembarked, Pridon said, "We should travel by night and rest by day. We need stealth now as much as we need speed."

After two nights of travel, they came within sight of the Kadji city. Its walls were massive, guarded by thousands of soldiers, and in the center rose the rock upon which Nestan's tower had been built. Tariel, Avtandil, and Pridon took counsel together about how best to assail the city and rescue Nestan. Each had a bold plan in mind, but in the end, Tariel's plan was the one they chose. Each man took with him a hundred soldiers, and each approached the city from a different side. It did not matter that they were badly outnumbered; each man fought with the ferocity of a hundred men, and none fought more fiercely than Tariel.

Avtandil and Pridon fought their way to the foot of the tower. Dead and dying guards lay everywhere, their armor rent, their blood flowing over the stones.

"Where is Tariel?" Avtandil asked.

Pridon pointed at the shattered tower door as an answer. "He is already inside. Only Tariel could have opened the door like that."

The two companions went inside and climbed the stairs, alert for enemies, but found none. When they got to the top of the stairs, there they found Tariel and Nestan-Daredjan, entwined in a long embrace. Tariel realized that they were not alone. He looked at his two companions and beamed.

"Look, my friends! The sun has returned to my day!" Tariel introduced his friends to Nestan-Daredjan.

All embraced and wept tears of joy.

The battle done, Pridon gave a proper burial to those of his men who had fallen in battle. Of the three hundred who left Pridon's land, only one hundred and sixty still lived. Then the knights and soldiers went through the town and slew every last foe. They gathered up all the treasure they could find, and in the end, they needed three thousand mules and camels to carry it all. Leaving sixty men to guard the looted city, they placed Nestan-Daredjan in a palanquin and rode for Gulansharo, where they intended to show their gratitude to the king and Patman, without whose aid Nestan would never have been found.

The Wedding of Tariel and Nestan-Daredjan

Tariel summoned a messenger and said, "Go to the king of the sea, who rules in Gulansharo. Invite him to meet us and be our guest. Tell him that we have sacked Kadjeti. That city is now his to rule, and the treasure it holds is his. Ask him also to bring Patman with him. We have rescued the one she holds dear, and we must put her fears to rest."

When the king of the sea learned of the deeds those brave knights had performed, he gladly assented to meet Tariel and his companions and agreed to have Patman accompany him. He rode out in train with Patman, his court, and his servants, and with mules laden with many precious gifts to give his hosts. The king was received with much joy by Pridon, Tariel, and Avtandil, and Patman and Nestan-Daredjan embraced and wept tears of joy.

"I never thought I would see you again. May God bless the ones who restored you to me," Patman said.

"And may God bless you, who is like a mother to me. When last you saw me, I was broken, but lo! Now I am whole, for the sun has been restored to my day," Nestan said.

The king of the sea's servants set up many bright pavilions, and the three friends exchanged costly gifts with him.

The king of the sea said to Tariel and Nestan, "There is no greater joy than to see two lovers united. It is my wish that you celebrate your wedding here with me, and there would be no greater honor to me than if you gave your assent."

So, it was that Tariel and Nestan-Daredjan plighted their troth, and the feasting, music, and dancing went on without stint for many days and nights.

Finally, it came time for the brave companions to depart. Again, they gave gifts to the king of the sea, and he presented them with many fine things. For Pridon and Avtandil there were the king's best horses, with tack and caparisons, and Tariel and Nestan were given jeweled crowns and bolts of the finest silk. The king also gave them a ship to take them home, and Tariel bowed humbly before the king in gratitude.

Soon it was time for farewells.

Tariel said to Patman, "I have not enough thanks to give to the one who is like a mother to my beloved Nestan. The best I can do is to give to you these jewels, pearls, and silks, which I hope you will take in recompense."

"O knight, my gratitude to you also knows no bounds. I am glad to have met you, and my heart rejoices for you and my dear Nestan, but I will be sad to see you go," Patman said.

Tariel said to the king of the sea, "Now we must depart for our lands. You will forever be as a father to us."

All of the friends embraced and shed bitter tears. Then the three brave companions and the lovely Nestan-Daredjan took ship and sailed for Pridon's land. They sent a messenger ahead to tell Asmat what had befallen and let Pridon's men know that their king was returning home unscathed. The companions rode in great joy to Pridon's castle, laughing and singing all the way, with Nestan-Daredjan carried in a beautiful palanquin so that she might make the journey unwearied.

The road to Pridon's castle was lined with cheering people. Asmat came running, and as soon as Nestan saw her, she jumped down from her palanquin and went to embrace her beloved sister.

"Never did I think to see you alive again. May God forever bless the ones who brought you back to me," Asmat said.

"I have heard how you tended my dear Tariel in the time of his grief and yours. How can I ever repay you?" Nestan said.

"It is payment enough to see my brother and sister in their happiness."

With those whose kinsmen had been killed in the battle, Tariel and Avtandil also wept.

"Their lives were given for my life, and that I'll not forget. May God look graciously upon them and bring them to rest with him in his kingdom forever," Tariel said.

Pridon caused another wedding feast to be held for Tariel and Nestan-Daredjan, and the whole palace made merry for eight full days.

At the end of the festivities, Tariel said to Pridon, "I ask a favor of you. Go to Avtandil and ask him what I might do for him since he has done so much for me."

Pridon went to Avtandil and gave him Tariel's message.

"There is nothing Tariel can do for me. I have wealth enough for any man, a liege lord who I am happy to serve, and when my beloved deems fit, her I shall wed. I wish only for Tariel's prosperity and happiness and to see him sit upon the throne of India," Avtandil replied.

Pridon reported Avtandil's reply to Tariel.

"I see. He is both proud and generous, but I'll not be thwarted. Tell him that I want to visit Rostevan, to ask forgiveness for having killed his men, and to ask Tinatin's hand for Avtandil," Tariel said.

Pridon again went to Avtandil and delivered Tariel's message. Avtandil's heart was wrung by Tariel's offer.

He went to Tariel himself and knelt before him. "Tariel, my dearest friend and brother, do not go to Rostevan. I've caused him enough grief, and I'll not be responsible for more. Nor shall I increase my beloved's woe since surely she blames me for Rostevan's unhappiness. If you remind them of that fateful day, their sorrow surely will increase."

"Never fear. I go to Rostevan as one king to another to pay my respects. That at least is courtesy, and I'll say what I need to say in the most diplomatic terms. May I ask for his daughter's hand to be given to one who is dearer to me than any brother? That is a request that one king may make of another, surely."

"To that, I will assent," Avtandil said.

The Wedding of Avtandil and Tinatin

The three brave companions left Pridon's realm and made for Tariel's cave, bearing Nestan-Daredjan and Asmat in a beautiful palanquin, accompanied by many of Pridon's soldiers. On the way, they hunted game, and when they got to the cave, the soldiers made their own camp nearby and cooked their meals, while inside the cave, Asmat roasted the meat for herself and her friends. The five friends had a merry meal together, and the place that once was the home of deep sorrow was now full of joy and laughter. When the meal was done, they explored the rest of the cave, and there they found even more treasure than they had thought possible to be collected in one place. Tariel and Nestan-Daredjan saw to it that all of Pridon's soldiers and generals were generously rewarded, and still, there was a great quantity of wealth remaining.

"My lord Pridon, I owe you a deep debt for your aid in finding my dear Nestan. I, therefore, would like to give all the rest of this treasure to you, to do with as you see fit," Tariel said.

"I don't know how to thank you for this. All I can say is that this treasure will be no substitute for your presence at my court. Your friendship and valor I prize above all the gold and jewels the world has to offer," Pridon said.

Pridon sent some of his men to fetch camels to carry the riches from the cave, and in the morning, the five companions rode to Rostevan's kingdom with the soldiers who had stayed behind. As they rode through the villages of Arabia, they noticed that all the people were in mourning.

"Who has died?" Pridon asked.

"They mourn for me. They think me dead because they don't know that I have returned from my quest," Avtandil replied.

When the friends and their retinue had made camp, Tariel wrote a letter to King Rostevan and summoned a messenger to take it to the palace. Tariel wrote:

> To Rostevan, King of All Araby, from Tariel, King of India, greetings. My gracious King Rostevan, I write to you to as one king to another, on two accounts. On one fateful day many years ago, you sent out armed men to capture me, and I slew them. That was wrong of me, although equally was it wrong of you to assail me thus. But because of me, you suffered the loss of servants who were dear to you, and therefore, I beg your forgiveness. That is one

part of my message to you. The other is to bring you good tidings, for with me travels a knight who knows no peer and for whom I know you have great affection. Avtandil is here, come at last to the place that is his home and that he holds so dear.

When Rostevan read Tariel's letter, he shouted for joy. "Avtandil is home! No longer are we in mourning, for Avtandil has returned!"

Rostevan ordered his soldiers to saddle their mounts and go with him to greet Avtandil and conduct him and his friends to the palace with great pomp and rejoicing. He ordered drummers and musicians to come along and play cheerful, martial music all the way there and back. The soldiers all raced to do their king's bidding, for Avtandil was nearly as beloved to them as he was to Rostevan.

Tinatin, for her part, wept for joy that her dear Avtandil was returned to her.

Avtandil looked down the road toward the palace. He saw the great cloud of dust stirred up by Rostevan and his train and heard the faint sound of music and drums.

Avtandil went to Tariel and said, "I cannot meet Rostevan today. I am too ashamed of my disobedience. Let you and Pridon go and greet him first and see what his mood might be, and then send me news."

"Yes, that is proper. Never fear. We'll smooth the way for you," Tariel said.

Tariel and Pridon rode out to greet Rostevan, while Avtandil and Nestan-Daredjan stayed behind. Soon the kings met on the road. Seeing Tariel's beauty so smote Rostevan that he alit from his horse and bowed low to the younger man. Tariel likewise dismounted and bowed to Rostevan. The two kings embraced.

"My lord, will you sit with us in this meadow to converse?" Tariel asked.

Tariel and Rostevan seated themselves on the grass, and then Tariel said, "My lord Rostevan, I know that Avtandil is dearer to you than a son, but I must tell you that to me the world holds no one dearer than that brave knight, save my own Nestan-Daredjan. When I was on the brink of death, he saved me, and by his valor was my beloved returned to me. Avtandil has told me of his love for Tinatin. Therefore, I ask you on bended knee to grant your blessings to them and allow them to wed."

Then Tariel knelt before Rostevan and bowed low in supplication.

Rostevan was troubled by the way Tariel humbled himself.

Rostevan likewise knelt and bowed to Tariel, saying, "O valorous one, you needn't abase yourself for this request. No better son-in-law could I find than Avtandil, and my daughter has chosen him for her own. Tinatin is the wise ruler of this realm, and her judgment never falters."

Upon hearing Rostevan's reply, Pridon galloped back to the camp.

"Mount your horse! Come and meet Rostevan. He will grant all your desire," he told Avtandil.

Avtandil mounted and rode to the meadow with Pridon, his heart full of foreboding. He found Rostevan and Tariel standing there together, smiling. Avtandil dismounted, then threw himself on the ground and embraced Rostevan's feet.

"O my most gracious king, forgive me my disobedience. I did what I did only for love and not out of any wish to cause you sorrow."

Rostevan helped Avtandil to rise and embraced him. "Most valorous knight, dearer to me than any son, I am neither angered nor sorrowed by your deeds. I rejoice in them rather and would see you rejoicing, too, for today I give my blessing for you to wed our dearest Tinatin, who awaits you at the palace."

"I have no words to thank you. But before we ride to your palace, may we do one act of courtesy? Tariel's Nestan-Daredjan awaits us at our camp, and I wish that you would meet her and that she might accompany us on our return."

Rostevan gladly agreed, and when Nestan-Daredjan arose to greet him, he was smitten by her beauty and greeted her well as a king ought to do. Nestan mounted her palanquin and the knights their horses, and they all rode back to Rostevan's court with great rejoicing.

There they found Tinatin waiting, wearing her royal crown and bearing her scepter. Tariel and Nestan-Daredjan bowed before Tinatin, paid homage, and then led Tinatin to her throne. They took Avtandil by the hand and led him onto the dais to sit beside her.

Tinatin was overcome; she was pale and trembling.

Avtandil was robbed of speech and could do nothing but gaze at her.

Rostevan said, "My children, it is my heart's great delight to see you wed and rule wisely and well together when I am no more." Then he turned to his soldiers and vassals. "Here are your liege lords. Tinatin and Avtandil now rule this realm, and to them, you owe all fealty."

Tariel said to Tinatin, "How it gladdens my heart to see you united with he who is dearer than any brother. From this day forth, you shall be my sister, and I promise that always I will give you aid whenever you need it."

Rostevan commanded a great wedding banquet to be held for Tinatin and Avtandil. Every soldier received a gift, and Rostevan commanded that his treasury be opened and presents given to all the people according to their needs. To Pridon, Rostevan gave nine fiery steeds with saddles and tack, and to Tariel and Nestan, a great weight of gems and pearls.

The feasting and drinking went on without stint for many days. Such was the rejoicing that Tinatin and Avtandil, at last, were united.

All too soon, the celebrations came to an end.

Tariel went to Rostevan and said, "You have been the most exemplary host, and it gives me pain to have to leave your court. But my country has been overrun by enemies, and I must ride to save my kingdom."

"I weep to see you depart, but my armies are yours to command. Take my men and take back what is yours, and you and Nestan-Daredjan are forever welcome as my guests whenever you please to come," Rostevan said.

Pridon and Avtandil likewise pledged themselves to fight for Tariel, and soon they rode out at the head of Rostevan's army, whose numbers were swelled by the men Pridon had brought along.

Tinatin's parting with Nestan-Daredjan was bitter. They embraced and shed tears, pledging that they should be sisters forevermore.

Tariel, Pridon, and Avtandil took their leave of Rostevan, the valorous ones embracing the aged king with much affection. Tariel and Pridon pledged alliance with Rostevan, and Avtandil promised he would return as soon as Tariel had been restored to his throne.

The army wound its way from Arabia to India, and on the way, they met a group of Indian merchants whose heads were shorn and wore black, tattered clothing.

Tariel asked them, "Where are you from, and why are you dressed thus?"

"We are merchants from India. We wear mourning because our liege lord, Parsadan, is dead. What is worse is that Parsadan's daughter, whose loveliness rivals that of the sun, disappeared many years ago, and along with her Parsadan's most trusted knight. Seeing our realm in such disarray, the Khatavians attacked."

Hearing this, both Nestan-Daredjan cried out in grief. They wept and tore their hair at the news that Parsadan was dead.

"Woe to me!" Nestan cried.

"Alas, my father is dead! He who raised me as a son is no more! There is no light in my day!" Tariel cried.

"The queen yet lives, my lord and my lady," the merchants said, who now recognized Tariel and Nestan, "and our army still fights, but they are weary and outnumbered and besieged. We see that you have many men. Ride to the aid of our country! Overthrow King Ramaz and his men! Save our beloved queen!"

Tariel and his companions hastened to the field of battle. They saw the might of the Khatavian army but were not dismayed. Tariel sent some men to capture the Khatavian sentries, with orders that are brought back alive. Soon they were brought before Tariel, where they cast themselves at his feet and begged for mercy.

"I'll not slay you. Instead, I send you back to your king with a message. Tell Ramaz that Tariel is here, with the armies of Arabia, and with King Pridon and his men. Tell him that we'll gladly meet him on the field of battle but that he should prepare himself for defeat. Tariel is the rightful king of India and will spare no man in the slaughter to come. But if Ramaz is willing to surrender, he will be given safe-conduct, and we will use mercy toward him and his men," Tariel said.

Tariel sent the sentries back to Ramaz and then arrayed his army for battle. The standards of India, Arabia, and Mulghazanzar fluttered brightly in the wind. Seeing those three flags together made Ramaz's blood turn to water in his veins.

He went to Tariel and bowed low before him. "I surrender. Pride led me to invade when I saw that India was unprotected. I deserve to die for my presumption, I and all my viziers. But spare my soldiers. They are here because they were ordered to be and are innocent."

"I accept your surrender. You may go, and your soldiers will not be harmed. Do not raise a sword against us again, for next time, we will spare none of you," Tariel said.

Tariel rode to the fortress where the Indian army was besieged. At first, no one recognized him, but then he shouted, "It is I, Tariel, and I bring with me Nestan-Daredjan! We have returned!"

When the people realized who was outside the gate, they sent up a great cheer and sent out a party of soldiers to greet Tariel and his bride. Tariel and Nestan were reunited with the queen, and their tears of joy at their reunion were mixed with tears of sorrow for the passing of Parsadan. Avtandil and Pridon conveyed their condolences to the queen, who received those two knights with all the courtesy they deserved.

"Enough of your tears. Tariel and Nestan-Daredjan have returned to us. Let us have a feast to celebrate their union, and let them be set upon the throne of India," the queen said.

Tariel and Nestan were seated upon golden thrones, and at their side were Avtandil and Pridon.

Tariel summoned Asmat and said, "But for you, I would have perished. Any reward you ask for will be yours, and any man you wish to wed will be your husband."

"I wish nothing more than to continue to serve you and Nestan-Daredjan," Asmat said, and Tariel and Nestan received her service with much gratitude.

After many days of feasting and celebration, Avtandil went to Tariel and said, "My heart grieves to be parted from you, but my own Tinatin is waiting at home for me, and I would not have her sorrow. Alas, I must go."

Pridon said, "I must return to my land as well. Woe that I cannot stay. But I shall visit you as often as I may, and I beg you and Nestan-Daredjan often to be my guests at my own court."

Tariel gave Avtandil and Pridon many gifts, and Nestan gave Avtandil presents to give to Tinatin. The friends all embraced and wept as they said their farewells.

Pridon and his men rode with Avtandil and the Arabian army for a while, but then their paths parted, and each went to his own home.

So it was that Tariel was reunited with Nestan-Daredjan and that Avtandil wed Tinatin. These kings and queens ruled wisely and well and visited one another and their good friend King Pridon whenever possible. Their realms prospered under their care until the end of their lives.

Here's another book by Matt Clayton that you might like

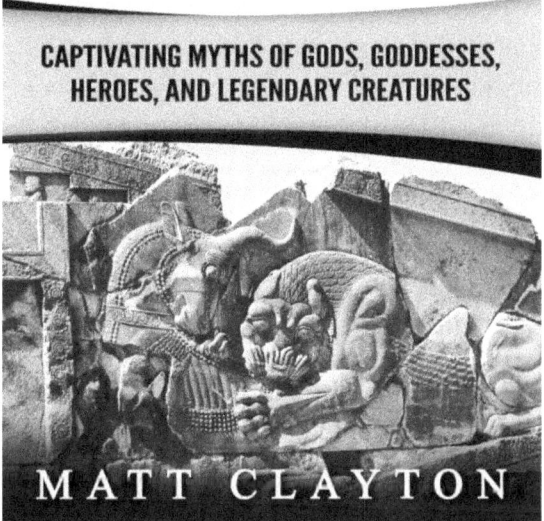

Free Bonus from Captivating History (Available for a Limited time)

Hi History Lovers!

Now you have a chance to join our exclusive history list so you can get your first history ebook for free as well as discounts and a potential to get more history books for free! Simply visit the link below to join.

Captivatinghistory.com/ebook

Also, make sure to follow us on Facebook, Twitter and Youtube by searching for Captivating History.

Bibliography

Arnot, Robert, and F.B. Collins, trans. *Armenian Literature*. New York: The Colonial Press, 1901.

Carpenter, Frances. *Wonder Tales of Horses and Heroes*. Garden City: Doubleday & Company, Inc., 1952.

Colarusso, John, trans. *Nart Sagas from the Caucasus: Myths and Legends from the Circassians, Abazas, Abkhaz, and Ubykhs*. Princeton: Princeton University Press, 2002.

Hedeghalh'e, Asker. *The Narts: Circassian Epos*. Vol. 1. Maikop: The Circassian Research and Science Institute, 1968). Excerpts translated by Amjad Jaimoukha, on the webpage *More Nart Tales*. <https://web.archive.org/web/20170113170919/http://www.reocities.com/Eureka/Enterprises/2493/nartsaga3.htm>. Accessed 21 January 2021.

Rustaveli, Shota. *The Knight in the Panther's Skin*. Translated by Lyn Coffin. Tbilisi: POEZIA Press, 2015.

Rust'haveli, Shot'ha. *The Man in the Panther's's Skin: A Romantic Epic*. Translated by Marjory Scott Wardrop. London: Royal Asiatic Society, 1912.

Seklemian, A. G. *The Golden Maiden and Other Folk Tales and Fairy Stories Told in Armenia*. Cleveland: The Helman-Taylor Company, 1898.

Shalian, Artin K., trans. *David of Sassoun: The Armenian Epic in Four Cycles*. Athens, OH: Ohio University Press, 1964.

Sideman, Belle Becker. *The World's Best Fairy Tales*. Pleasantville: The Reader's Digest Association, 1967.

Tolegian, Aram. "David of Sassoun: The Armenian Folk Epic." PhD diss., University of Southern California, 1960.

Toumanian, Hovhaness. "David of Sassoun." Translated by Thomas Samuelian. Arak29. Accessed 25 January, 2021. https://arak29.org/david-of-sassoon/

Tvirdíková, Michaela. *Folk Tales and Legends*. Translated by Vira Gissing. London: Cathay Books, 1981.

www.ingramcontent.com/pod-product-compliance
Lightning Source LLC
Chambersburg PA
CBHW050513240426
43673CB00004B/202